The Spiritual Fragrance Of A Woman

A Fragrance That Attracts The Right Man

By
Jerone L. Davison

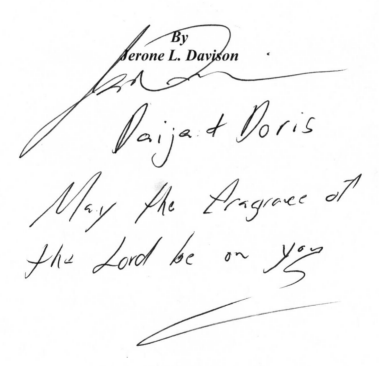

Paija & Doris

May the Fragrance of
the Lord be on you

www.spiritualfragrance.org

Requests for permission to make copies of any part of this work should be mailed to Permissions Department, Witty Writings Publishing, LLC. 2875-F Northtowne Ln. #232, Reno, NV. 89512

ISBN: 978-0-9785571-3-1

Printed in the United States of America by Witty Writings Press

Forward

The Spiritual Fragrance of a Woman
The Fragrance That Attracts the Right Man

This book is designed to give insight, power, and instruction to women who are single and searching. Far too many single women are in the church, and this displeases the heart and purpose of God. Large numbers of women in the church have been forced to live the single life because of the circumstances that a sin-filled society produces. Singleness in the church has now reached unbelievable statistical levels; sowing a spirit of panic and hopelessness in the hearts and minds of single members has increased sexual immorality in the church as well. God's women are being robbed of the opportunity to be found, married and loved for a lifetime due to lack of knowledge and several male factors such as unfaithfulness, immaturity, homosexuality, incarceration, premature death and promiscuous women. Many single women are beginning to throw up their hands and give up on men altogether, using alterative ways to comfort themselves or resigning to live out their days in pain and frustration. The Spiritual Fragrance of a Woman is a powerful end-times revelation for the single woman. It doesn't have to be this way because God has a plan to equip you for the blessing of marriage.

In his book Pastor Jerone Davison uses the authority and anointing of a father to give instruction. He gives the reader several reasons why a good woman may not attract good men. He also exposes why good women continue to attract bad men, uncovering a defect in their aroma. He teaches the gift and anointing of a spiritual fragrance are God-given keys that will make the difference in getting into and maintaining a good relationship.

Pastor Jerone builds his biblical teaching from the book the Song of Solomon and exposes the secret fragrance of the Shulammite woman, the wife of King Solomon. This book illustrates the key to attracting good men is to have a fragrance designed by Jesus the Perfume Maker. The Shulammite woman was anointed with nine fragrances used to draw

4

Solomon to her town and into her life. The reader will see from the scriptures the meaning of the fragrances and how to become anointed with each of them.

The Spiritual Fragrance of a Woman is biblically based sound teaching with charts and questionnaires that will aid the reader in grasping this revelation and life-changing concept.

About The Author

Pastor Jerone L. Davison spent several years in the NFL with the Oakland Raiders and the San Francisco 49ers. He is an anointed Preacher, Teacher, Conference Host and Speaker. Jerone is a Family and Relationship Specialist with extensive training and experience in both disciplines. He is also a Certified Parenting Instructor, Creative Conflict Resolution Facilitator, Anger Management Instructor and Marriage and Family Counselor. Pastor Davison is gifted with wisdom in the Word of God and deliverance often accompanies his ministry. He is the Senior Pastor/Founder of a growing congregation in Fairfield, California, the Bountiful Harvest Church.

Pastor Davison is a graduate of Solano College with an AA in Science Degree and received a higher degree of study in Sociology from Arizona State University. He also holds a BA in Biblical Studies in Biblical Preaching and is now studying for his MA in Biblical Counseling with plans to receive a DD of Divinity in the near future.

Jerone Davison is a dynamic man of God in whom the Spirit of Praise, Power, Prayer and Prophetic Speech rests upon. His messages center on the Redemptive Work of Christ in all facets of life, including relationships.

He is the proud husband of Sharon Wynn-Davison for over fifteen years, and father to their five children; four girls and a boy (whom he lovingly calls his only begotten son) Janay, Jashe', Jada, Jerone Jr. and Jaya (arranged from oldest to youngest).

The Spiritual Fragrance Of A Woman
The Fragrance That Attracts The Right Man

TABLE OF CONTENTS

Introduction

I was asked by a local gospel radio personality in Northern California to conduct a teaching series for single women. When I accepted, the Spirit of the Lord told me to teach on "The Spiritual Fragrance of a Woman." The radio station aired the four-minute segments throughout the day and the next day would continue with another part of the teaching, and so forth. The response was unbelievable. Women from all over the Bay Area in Northern California were calling the radio station asking for more information about myself, my church, and the topic 'Spiritual Fragrance of a Woman'. People would see me in the grocery store and ask for the tape, a book, or something, but I had nothing tangible to give them. Several members of my church came to me and said, "Pastor if you do a conference we will pay the cost". Some said, "We will pass out flyers door-to-door, whatever it takes, because women need to hear what God has given you". The most surprising part of it all is men and even Pastors have asked me for a DVD, CD, book or tape on the Spiritual Fragrance of a Woman.

The Spirit of the Lord let me know it was time to put the teaching in written form and begin to restore hurting and aspiring women to receive His anointed fragrances, to bear fruit and the gifts of the Spirit through our resources and conferences. This revelation will not only bring discretion back into the lives of women but it will bless the ones who are seeking godly relationships. This book (teaching) has an anointing for holy matrimony. Singles will get married and their lonely days will be as a moment when the Lord fulfills His word to rise up men to be husbands to the faithful in His house.

Read this prophetic word found in the book of Isaiah:

> *"Sing, O childless woman! Break forth into loud and joyful song, O Jerusalem, even though you never gave birth to a child. For the woman who could bear no children now has more than all the other women," says*

the LORD. [2]*"Enlarge your house; build an addition; spread out your home!* [3] *For you will soon be bursting at the seams. Your descendants will take over other nations and live in their cities".*

Isaiah 54:1-3 (New Living Translation)

Everyone needs and deserves to have a meaningful relationship with a significant other, a husband who loves the Lord and is serious about fulfilling God's plan for his life. God said it's not good for man to be alone. Out of the six "goods" and one "very good" noted (Genesis 1), there was only one "not good". When we look at Genesis 2:18 we find the not good and it is tied to Adam's relationship or lack of thereof with another person. So why are so many Christians single; searchers who end up with no one or the wrong one? Could you be suffering from a Spiritual Fragrance Disorder? Are you missing something? Why are so many good women attracting bad men? This book will answer those questions and much more.

It is my truest desire that this book will feed you with knowledge, deliver where deliverance is needed, mentor and walk you through some hard, lonely and hurting places. I pray it teaches you the value of **you** and your walk with Christ while helping to draw a true man of God into your life forever in Holy Matrimony. Amen.

Acknowledgements

I am truly honored to be the vessel that the Lord Jesus has used to bring the revelation of the Spiritual Fragrance. It has been a great challenge for me to complete this book because I have the privilege of carrying so many others duties as a Husband, father of five, a son, friend of many, Pastor of a growing flock, and Spiritual Father to sons and daughters everywhere. As if those weren't enough, I still have to get to the gym and throw some weights around and play basketball to maintain my health and fitness level.

I give glory to God the Father for His manifold wisdom and His Mighty Plans for us and to Jesus Christ our Savior and Redeemer (what a man, I want to be just like HIM) a willing Sacrifice and a Leader. Thanks to the Holy Ghost (my Comforter, my Power Source, my Guide and my Friend) who is in us and on us forevermore. I thank Him for the grace He has provided me in completing this assignment for the Church.

Thanks to the Church of God In Christ for the beautiful training in Holiness, Prayer, Bible Study, Praise, Warfare, Brotherhood and Loyalty to Jesus. It was God in you that rescued my family from destruction. Giving Honor to our Founder, the late, Bishop Charles H. Mason, and thanks to Bishop Albert Galbrath of Northern California First Jurisdiction for his support (my Bishop). Thanks to General Board Member Bishop Jerry Macklin for supporting me. Thanks to the late Supt. Harold Johnson Sr. whose wisdom and advice I still cherish and to his wife, Mother Johnson and to the entire Johnson family.

Thanks to my very Beautiful, Lovely, Gifted and Spiritually Perfumed Wife (Sharon Wynn-Davison). Sharon has had my back for a long time. She is my best friend and I can always count on her to be there for me. She recorded her debut album in 2005 entitled *"Favor"*. It is a must-have because of its fresh sound and anointed lyrics; it is awesome. She is a wonderful and faithful wife, graceful, a wise counselor, an encourager, a helper, and is a highly anointed and blessed woman of the Lord. I love her very much. *Jerone & Sharon 4ever.*

Thanks and love to my five children Janay my oldest, Jashe' second, Jada third, Jerone Jr. fourth and Jaya my last. To my four beautiful girls, Daddy prays for you always that God will bless you with good husbands. You are God's girls and I am blessed He gave you to me so I would have the privilege of raising you to love *Him*. To my only son, boy you don't have a choice, you're going to be a good man, a good husband, and a preaching prophet. Young man of God, I love you. Be a faithful SEED CARRIER.

Thanks to my mother, Janice Travis-Davison, who taught me to pray and love God. She was and is instrumental in my development into the faith of Jesus the Son of God, manhood and marriage. She is a mighty woman of prayer, wisdom and faith. Thank you Mama for everything; you are awesome. Thanks to my dad, Johnny, for being dad (you know). Thanks to my only sister and her husband, my brother-in-law for being there. Love to Aunt Jean and to Aunt Blondean, thanks for taking me in. You were a refuge to me; we're praying for you. To my two brothers just for being my brothers. Much love to my mother-in-law, my mama, thanks for the encouragement, love and prayers through the years and thank you for raising such a good and beautiful woman to be my wife. Thanks to all my sisters in law, The Wynns, to John and my other brothers-in-law. Thanks to Aunt Tee Robbye and Aunt Tee Doris.

Thanks to the Bountiful Harvest Church Family. I am proud of you BHC. You are so much fun and a joy for me to pastor; I love you with all my heart. You are a great people with limitless potential and ability. God's favor and blessing are on you. Thank you for your prayers, encouragement, and support.

Thanks to my folks, Nate DuPree and Tim Holloway at Witty Publishing. Awesome work and cook fellowship. Thanks to Kerri Holloway for her patience and skill and for going the extra mile with the editing (because I had to start all over). Thanks for the encouragement.

Thanks to churches across the nation for the open door and thanks to you dear reader for purchasing this book and for taking the time to read the heart of the man of God, the Spiritual Father to the fatherless. May God add a blessing to you as you read the revelation He gave to me for you. As one who has been given the keys of the Kingdom I bind all things that are lustful or even closely related to lust from every reader and hearer of this book and I loose the Spirit of True Love upon you in Jesus' name, and it is so.

Chapter 1

Smells Are Attractive

*A*ll smells no matter how delightful or how dreadful are attractive to someone or something. Some smells entice with a sweet aroma and others attract attention with a foul odor. Things that smell good to you may be unbearable to others and vice versa. The purpose of this book is to help you realize that God has given you an aroma to assist you in relationships. For instance, your faith, words, behavior, and actions determine whether your aroma is attractive or not.

To illustrate the importance of smell let's begin with the animal kingdom. God has placed an open mystery in their behavior as an example of a spiritual truth. Bees are drawn to flowers powdered by the main ingredient for their honey (pollen). The Humming Bird is lured to the succulent smell of sweet nectar in plants and fruit. Buzzards are summoned from far distances by the smell of decayed carcasses and the stench of death. Sharks are so sensitive they can taste a drop of blood in the ocean from over fifty miles away. Ants will march all over your house for the tiniest drop of sugar.

Most male animals can smell when the female of their species has come into full season and is ready to mate. A bull weighing 2,500 pounds will fight or even kill anything in its path to get to a heifer in heat. Male deer can pick up the scent of a female from her urine, which signals she is ready for mating. This is when the fields become full of bucks jockeying for position to be the one to mate with her. All of these activities take place because of the scent of the female. No, this is not a lesson on animal behavior but it is a lesson on the power of odor and smell. I simply want you to understand these natural things are expressions of the spiritual order of God.

Smells Are Attractive

Are you ready for a mate? Have you allowed Jesus to mold and shape you into what He wants you to be or are you bringing in the men *you* want? Have you said yes to the Lord while you wait?

The only wise God is revealing two very powerful yet unrealized keys to finding a meaningful relationship. These two gifts of God are odor and smell. As you may have noticed in some of the examples given above, the female always gave off the scent to attract the male, and the male had the sense of smell to locate her. The female has a major role to play in attracting the male. Her body must be functioning properly without any defects. The scent that comes from her body needs the aroma of good health; otherwise the male will not mate with her because he wants his offspring to have a healthy, nurturing mother. It is the same with you, the spiritual female. Your spiritual perfume has to smell of the right ingredients and cannot be defected with personal issues, fears, failures, soul-ties, etc. If so, your defected aroma may ultimately chase him away.

Smell is the key that unlocks the majestic beauty and instincts of the animal kingdom. Thus we see smell is a powerful gift to earthly creatures that aids in attracting and finding mates whose timing and destiny is aligned with theirs.

The Bible says nature shows us the wisdom and the mind of God. If the natural kingdom is dominated by odor and smell, then how much more the spiritual kingdom? Follow me closely as we explore and explain the power of scent and smell.

> [19] *Because that which may be known of God is manifest in them; for God hath shewed it unto them.* [20] *For the* **invisible** *things of him from the creation of the world are clearly seen, being understood by the things that are made (natural), even his* **eternal** *(spiritual) power and Godhead; so that they are without excuse:*
>
> *Romans 1:19-20 (KJV)*

> [45] *The Scriptures tell us, "The first man, Adam, became a living person." But the last Adam—that is, Christ—is a*

17

Smells Are Attractive

life-giving Spirit. [46] *What came* **first was the natural body, then the spiritual body comes later.**

1 Corinthians 15:45-46 (New Living Translation)

Without the woman's spiritual fragrance and the man's spiritual and prophetic ability to smell, relationships will shut down as they are doing now because the two cannot sense the Holy Spirit. It is next to impossible to find a spiritual soul mate without the aid of the Spirit. You both need spiritual tools in order to find each other. Not only will the Spirit lead you to the right person but He will let you know when the time is right to commit to the covenant of marriage in conjunction with biblical counseling.

Relationships and marriages are becoming nothing more than a business partnership with an "I help you and you help me" attitude. Many marriages lack meaning, purpose, joy and real love because they are unequally yoked. People have forsaken the wisdom and ability of the Spirit and have gone Hollywood as they search for a mate to marry or to live with. If the woman is not anointed with the fragrant oil of the Lord and the man has no spiritual ability to smell the two will not come together as one. People are just hooking up only to get hooked up, hoping to gain something tangible like sex, money, a place to live, children, car or clothing. This is not the will of God. Few look for purpose, meaning, a future, righteousness, peace, a lifelong commitment, direction or pleasing the heart of God with a holy relationship.

We can't just hook up with anybody. That type of behavior puts us on a lower scale than the animals. When animals come together they do so with purpose because of their gift of smell. A female in the animal kingdom will not let just any male come near her but she will invite the strongest one because she is thinking of her offspring, their security and their future. The man and the woman were made higher than the animals (Genesis 1:28) and a *little* lower than the angels (Psalm 8:4-6). Our placement and position in God's creation lets us know mankind is the cream of the crop in the earth and if anyone or anything should operate with purpose it should be us. If we are going to repair and restore the relationship between

Smells Are Attractive

man and woman then we must allow the Spirit of Jesus to anoint our sense of smell and bless us with the gifts, fruit and perfumes that will draw men and women together in Holy Matrimony.

God Desires Fellowship

Smell is so important to God that He prepared the earth for His visitation by perfuming the Garden of Eden so when He entered it to commune with Adam He would *smell* heaven on earth.   The fragrance was named bdellium (Genesis 2:12). It was the color of manna (Numbers 11:7) that fell from heaven to feed Israel in the wilderness. Manna was a type of bread used as a sign of fellowship. During Old Testament times there was a table of shewbread or the bread of His presence that the priests were ordered to set before the face of God (Exodus 25:30). God plus bread equals *fellowship*. Jesus said He was the bread that came down from heaven.

> [48] *I am that bread of life.* [49] *Your fathers did eat manna in the wilderness, and are dead.* [50] *This is the bread which cometh down from heaven, that a man may eat thereof, and not die.* [51] *I am the living bread which came down from heaven: if any man eat of this bread, he shall live for ever: and the bread that I will give is my flesh, which I will give for the life of the world.*
>
> *John 6:48-51 (KJV)*

Thus bdellium is the blessed fragrance of fellowship, a symbol of peace between God and man. This was an important scent, which signaled the Lord with a sweet aroma, welcoming God into His garden. It was there in the midst of the bdellium trees and the beautiful aroma that God and man had sweet fellowship. God is always looking to fellowship with man but there must be a sweet aroma present. That sweet aroma is none other than Jesus Christ the Righteous One who gave Himself as a sweet smelling sacrifice for us.

Men love fellowship. Think about it. We huddle up in groups like schoolboys; we play sports together and watch sports together. It's enjoyable to us because of the fellowship. That's something many women don't know about men. We love to have someone to share a laugh, watch a game and pull for different teams in friendly competition.

If you had the anointing of bdellium (fellowship) it would make you very attractive to a good man that is looking for someone to share the rest of his life. If bdellium was good enough to draw God into the Garden of Eden to fellowship with Adam then the bdellium anointing will be more than good enough for one of God's sons.

Prophetic Smell

The ability to smell is a blessing. It is probably the most underrated of all of the senses, though it is the foundational sense the others are built upon. When God formed man from the dust he had a body but no spirit, no soul, no conscience, no sight, no thought, no memory, no hearing, no touch, no movement, no smell and no taste. It wasn't until God breathed into his nostrils (nose) that man became conscious and able to do all of the things mentioned above. Thus we see the importance and value God placed on the nose, making the natural and spiritual sense of smell the foundation of life.

When God breathed life into Adam He did it through his nose making it a spiritual place. It is the place where life comes in and where life goes out. An abundance of revelation is connected to the nose of a man. If he is alive in Christ then he can smell the very attractive fragrance of Christ flowing from you. Therefore you must be sure to radiate that spiritual fragrance on a daily basis.

Why did God breathe into Adam's nostrils the breath of life? This action is in sharp contrast to CPR (Cardiopulmonary Resuscitation) of which I am certified. In CPR training you are taught to plug the nose, tilt the head back and blow into the mouth. Not so with God and his creation called Adam (the Hebrew name for Adam is man). Why didn't He breathe into Adam's mouth instead? I believe the act of blowing into his nose was primarily to bring the nose to our attention, and secondly to show us the spiritual significance of the nose.

Smells Are Attractive

The Hebrew word for nose or nostril is ***Ap'.*** It is the origin of breathing and is also used for the human face. To the Jews breath in the nostrils was a sign of life so when they mentioned nostril everyone knew it meant life. *Ap'* also means the origin of smell but it is mostly used in Hebrew teaching as the location of emotion (Psalm 18:8), especially anger.

Back in the day when a boy really liked a girl the older folks would say the girl had his nose open "wide enough to drive a truck through."

That's what your aroma does. It widens his nose.

Once God breathed into him Adam became a living soul, one who could smell, taste, see, hear and touch the beauty of God's creation. That's exactly what you are my sister. You are God's creation, blossoming with beauty, a sweet fragrance, life giving waters, an oasis in the wilderness with trees bearing delicious fruit, of which a dead man cannot taste nor smell, neither should he. Only a living man can truly enjoy the creation of God. He appreciates the value of your fragrance and fruit and how to enjoy them. He knows how precious life is and how beautiful the life of God is in you. When Adam was given the responsibility of naming the animals he never said "woman" to any of them. God put him to sleep, removed a rib from his side, formed Eve and brought her before him and then he said, "wo-man", meaning she was taken out of man.

Adam had a physical nose but it couldn't enjoy spiritual perfumes. The only way a physical nose becomes a spiritual nose is when the Life of God is blown into that person. Who is God? God is a Spirit and they that worship Him must worship Him in spirit and in truth. Therefore when God (who is a Spirit) blows the breath of life, the man's nose and spirit become spiritually alive and sensitive to spiritual things. This action taken by God revealed everything Adam was going to do would be based on his sense of smell, not by sight. As I stated before, without breath in the nose Adam just laid there and so it is in the Spirit. When we can't smell in the Spirit we are inoperable in the spirit realm and in some cases in the natural realm as well (Psalm 115:6). Smelling in the Spirit is what I have coined to be prophetic smell. **Prophetic smell is having a connection and sensitivity to the Spirit of the Lord by way of spiritual smell.** Just as there are five senses in the natural likewise there are five prophetic sense gifts. I will highlight them as they are connected to our five natural senses.

The Five Prophetic Senses

Sight   (I Samuel 9:9, II Kings 6:17)
Hearing   (I Kings 18:41, Revelation 2:7)
Touch   (Acts 21:10-11, II Kings 13:21, Matthew 9:20-22)
Taste   (Psalm 34:8 , Hebrews 2:9, Luke 14:24)
Smell   (Joel 2:20, II Corinthians 2:15-16)

All of these are the spiritual counterparts of our natural senses.

As you can see God has not left himself without a witness. He has various ways to ensure His people receive knowledge from the Spirit. Prophetic Smell is in operation even today yet it must be relied upon now more than any other time, especially when it comes to finding a potential mate. We shouldn't simply depend on fleshly senses to guide us in such an important life decision. We must place the greatest value on the wisdom of the Spirit of God to bring to pass His will for our lives by using the gifts of the Spirit to aid us in life's affairs.

It was prophetic smell that led a Prophetess to bind the spirit of cancer in a woman during a worship service, after smelling the diseased aroma coming from the woman's body, and she was healed. People around the world are walking in their gift and smell the spirit of fear, stress, doubt, oppression and possession. They can smell the presence of the Lord and when Angels are present; smelling blessings, anointing, joy, prosperity and so much more. The power of prophetic smell has been overlooked. In these last days it is essential for us to wake up and call upon this gift to strengthen us again, especially for godly relationships.

Prophetic smell is being heightened in men who are alive to God and are spending time in the presence of the Lord Jesus, asking to be led by His Spirit. Once they receive life from the Spirit they will be looking for wives. I believe a specific man's prophetic sense of smell is being turned

Smells Are Attractive

on just for you and he will be drawn to your own unique aroma from Jesus. As you put on more of fragrances of the Lord the stronger your scent will be for him to pick up and soon find you.

It is your assignment to get yourself in the right position to be blessed and anointed with the perfume of The Spirit of the Lord. Trust that God will heighten your spiritual fragrance and direct it toward the man He has prepared for you. I don't know about your particular situation nor do I know what you've been told. I am persuaded the order and the plan of God is for man and woman to be joined together in a holy union, not living single and hating it (Genesis 2:18). I am not saying you cannot be happy as a single Christian, many are, but I wonder if it is only because of fear, past failures or bad examples.

You must trust the Lord. Do you trust Him? Do you realize the anointed aroma on you is for more than shouting, dancing and speaking in tongues? It is also an anointing for relationships. I cannot tell you where he is coming from but I do know your anointed fragrance will draw him to you.

God your Father wants you to be married. I am a father of four girls; one just became a teen and even I desire for my daughters to be married (Luke 11:13). My wife and I are celebrating fifteen years of marriage and five children. The church members under our leadership are being blessed in their marriages and singles are getting married because of the anointed aroma coming down from us.

Remember I said in the beginning of this chapter that all smells attract attention. Could your smell be the reason why the wrong types of men are coming to you? Something about the way you smell spiritually attracts certain men to you. I want you to understand God is LORD of all, even over the realm of scents. God is faithful not to forget you. He knows what you need and what you desire; He will meet them both. If God has done it for others He will do it for you.

Smells Are Attractive

Test Your Spiritual Fragrance

List nine reasons why odor and smell are important in the natural and the spiritual:

1.

2.

3.

4.

5.

6.

7.

8.

9.

Chapter 2

The Spiritual Fragrance of a Woman

[13] Thy plants are an orchard of pomegranates, with pleasant fruits; camphire, with spikenard, [14] Spikenard and saffron; calamus and cinnamon, with all trees of frankincense; myrrh and aloes, with all the chief spices:

Song of Solomon 4:13-14 (KJV)

The question is how did you get your field full of bulls, bucks and rams? How do you as a woman who loves the Lord attract a man of God into your life even though there seems to be a shortage of God-loving, spirit-led and spirit-baptized men? The answer lies in the type of Spiritual Fragrance you wear. The Spiritual Fragrances of a woman are: the nine fragrances in Song of Solomon 4:13, the Fruits of the Spirit found in Galatians 5:22 and the Gifts of the Spirit in I Corinthians 12:7-11. You may be attractive, but are you anointed? You may be educated, but are you anointed? Don't simply depend on natural attributes but seek spiritual attributes as well. The spiritual scent is not something that can be purchased at the mall. It is not something you can spray on, rather it is something that comes from above.

You received your spiritual fragrance the moment you gave your life to the Lord. As you follow Jesus' Word day by day and walk with Him more closely over time you will become more anointed with the Spiritual Fragrance of a Woman (John 8:31). Natural perfume holds no comparison because the perfume you spray on your physical body may very well attract a man, but what kind of man? What type of man has your natural perfume drawn in the past? Natural men cannot smell and enjoy your spiritual perfume because it came from the Spirit of the Lord, which they

25

The Spiritual Fragrance of a Woman

cannot see, hear or comprehend. On the other hand, a spiritual man can smell you from across the globe because spiritual things are revealed to those who are in the spirit.

> *⁹ But as it is written, Eye hath not seen, nor ear heard, neither have entered into the heart of man, the things which God hath prepared for them that love him. ¹⁰ But God hath revealed them unto us by his Spirit: for the Spirit searcheth all things, yea, the deep things of God. ¹¹ For what man knoweth the things of a man, save the spirit of man which is in him? even so the things of God knoweth no man, but the Spirit of God. ¹² Now we have received, not the spirit of the world, but the Spirit which is of God; that we might know the things that are freely given to us of God. ¹³ Which things also we speak, not in the words which man's wisdom teacheth, but which the Holy Ghost teacheth; **comparing spiritual things with spiritual. ¹⁴ But the natural man receiveth not the things of the Spirit of God: for they are foolishness unto him: neither can he know them, because they are spiritually discerned.***

> *I Corinthians 2:9-14 (KJV)*

Song of Solomon 4:11 records the words of praise from Solomon the man, Solomon the newlywed, the man who is in love with a beautiful dark skinned woman, a Shulammite. The name Shulammite is the feminine form of the name Solomon. Yes! Solomon. The same Solomon who asked and received great wisdom from God is the same Solomon who is enjoying the physical and spiritual blessing of open love with his new bride.

I like the fact the Bible does not hide these pictures of human nature from us but in fact opens wide the book so we can see. It is a blessing to read these things, otherwise how will we know the mind of God for us when it comes to having and maintaining a passionate marital relationship? Ladies please beware of men who are so heavenly-minded that they are no earthly good, being ashamed of having natural affections for a wife. Many

The Spiritual Fragrance of a Woman

wives of ministers, deacons, elders, pastors and bishops suffer from a lack of passionate love from such men who feel they are not being spiritual when they come together with their wives. The Bible admonishes the husband to be ravished always with her love Proverbs 5:18-19. Every man should be excited to see, taste, smell and experience the beauty of his wife. It is the will of God for husbands and wives to enjoy the pleasure of coming together in holy union. Why should we, the ones whom God gave the privilege and the right to enjoy sexual relations, stand by and complain about the world using sex in perverse ways? We should be so blessed in our marriages that we bring the world to intense jealousy and open shame.

The spiritual fragrance of a woman is composed of the nine things Solomon mentions of his Shulammite wife.

This woman had it together. Solomon says she is very fruitful, comparing her to a gated field of pomegranates trees lined up in perfect rows. Pomegranates are known for their sweet juice and many seeds, which speak of multiplication and bringing forth fruit in great abundance. He says that she smells like:

Camphire, *Spikenard*, *Saffron*, *Calamus* **and** *Cinnamon*, **with all the trees of** *Frankincense*; *Myrrh* **and** *Aloes*, **with all the** *Chief Spices*.

Solomon was excited (just like any other man would be) about how abundant her godly character was. Each spice mentioned represents the gifts of God in her. It was not just natural smell; it was a spiritual scent. When people interact with you what do they see, hear, smell and feel? Your spiritual scent should be something they can observe from near and far. I hope you can truly say you are a tree of righteousness planted of the Lord that bears fruit.

> [3] *And he shall be like a tree planted by the rivers of water, that bringeth forth his fruit in his season; his leaf also shall not wither; and whatsoever he doeth shall prosper.*
> *Psalm 1:3 (KJV)*

The Spiritual Fragrance of a Woman

[23] And he took the blind man by the hand, and led him out of the town; and when he had spit on his eyes, and put his hands upon him, he asked him if he saw ought. [24] And he looked up, and said, I see men as trees, walking.

Mark 8:23-24 (KJV)

The spiritual fragrance is made of **camphire**, **spikenard**, **saffron**, **calamus** and **cinnamon**, **frankincense**, **myrrh** and **aloes**, with all the **chief spices.** Each of these has a particular meaning, purpose and gift that come along with them. Aspire to have all nine. You may be blessed to have them all but some could be seriously under developed. We have plenty of people in church that can praise but don't pray. Many people love to prophesy but lack the gift of helps. Many like to have friendships with the opposite sex but don't know how to keep under control. These are just a few examples of an imbalanced person that needs Jesus the Apothecary (the Perfumer) to fix them up.

The spiritual fragrance of a woman is the beautiful aroma of one who lives a balanced, holy and purposeful life. It is the aroma of a godly character that is obvious to those around you. When others are stirring up mess, you bring peace. A woman anointed with the fragrance of the Lord gives answers to the confused and practices what she preaches. The woman who lives the life of the spiritually perfumed does so not by her own might or power, but by the Spirit of the Lord (Zechariah 4:6).

The spiritual fragrance is a compilation of nine godly behaviors, characteristics, fruits and gifts; all from the Spirit of the Lord. These spiritual spices individually don't give off very much fragrance at all. When you put all of them together they become the beautiful scent of the Lord. It is more than a smell. It is a ministry. Once you become married, you will be anointed to minister to your husband.

When I began my research for this book I became very interested in how each of the spices would smell to my natural nose so I ordered all of them. To my surprise some of them didn't have much smell at all while others

The Spiritual Fragrance of a Woman

were very strong. When I mixed all of them together it was a magnificent fragrance.

When people smell these spices placed on you by the Perfume Maker (Jesus Christ) your have a blessed aroma. A skilled perfumer must place them on you and that's who Jesus is, the Anointer (Exodus 30:25). These nine fragrant characteristics are to be lived out and balanced out or else they will turn the beautiful fragrance into an obnoxious smell, which the Lord never intended.

Do not attempt to create your own spiritual spices because you don't how to apply the proper amounts of each fragrance. I think that is the mistake too many women make. They are so eager to move to the next page in their life so they mimic what other women are doing to get a man. Don't make that mistake. God's plan for you will not fit into their manmade schemes to 'hook' a man. Think back to the men you managed to catch in the past. I'm sure some of them you wish they'd never taken the bait. Those who care to be anointed must be careful to obey the leading of the Spirit in order for Him to mold and shape you in the places where you are weak and lacking. As one who likes to workout in the gym I notice many people working on areas of their body that are already strong but avoiding exercise techniques on areas that obviously need work, simply because it hurts.

Working on weak places always causes pain and fatigue because there is pressure to do or be something completely new. Jesus strengthens our weak places by allowing pressure to come and encouraging us to move closer to Him. The reward is worth the pain. You must be willing to go through to have a balanced fragrance with an attractive aroma.

Chapter 3

The Spiritual Scent Spa Rooms: Getting the Scent Massaged In

[13] Thy plants are an orchard of pomegranates, with pleasant fruits; camphire, with spikenard, [14] Spikenard and saffron; calamus and cinnamon, with all trees of frankincense; myrrh and aloes, with all the chief spices:

Song of Solomon 4:13-14 (KJV)

The Song of Solomon is a collection of songs considered to be the Holy of Holies of his 1,005 songs. These few selected songs are Solomon's very best and have so much to say and to teach us if only we were mature enough to receive it. It is a book full of symbols, pictures and spiritual images. In order for us to enjoy and appreciate them we must be spiritually mature and able to discern of the author's intent and message. It reveals how to live a committed single life and how to seek a soul mate God's way. Solomon's book can also demonstrate how to be faithful after finding a spouse. It teaches us about marriage and how to keep the passion therein. This book on godly relationships shows the wife how to excite her husband and the husband how to approach his wife with tenderness, affection and romance.

The sweet spices that made up the Shulammite woman's spiritual perfume are mentioned and celebrated by Solomon. He takes the time to name the spices individually as each one took on a separate meaning and led him into a different chamber or room. Her spices drew Solomon to her hometown where she worked in the hot sun and caught the attention of the handsome and wealthy king as he was checking on some of his property.

The Spiritual Scent Spa Rooms: Getting The Scent Massaged In

> [5] *I am black, but comely, O ye daughters of Jerusalem, as the tents of Kedar, as the curtains of Solomon.* [6] *Look not upon me, because I am black, because the sun hath looked upon me: my mother's children were angry with me; they made me the keeper of the vineyards; but mine own vineyard have I not kept.*
>
> *Song of Solomon 1:5-6 (KJV)*

Solomon was taken into a "spiritual love spa" to be covered in the natural and spiritual fragrance of his wife. Solomon sounded like a man in need of a vacation and romantic rendezvous; a place where he could be restored and renewed by the spiritual scent of his chosen bride.

He repeatedly mentioned escaping with her to a place called Lebanon, full of beautiful waterfalls and cool moist air. Lebanon was located in a high mountainous area surrounded by tropical plants, colorful flowers and tall trees good for shade from the hot desert sun. This high place depicts exactly what happens to a man who is intoxicated by the aroma of a spiritually perfumed woman. A good woman has the ability to lift a man to higher levels in life. It is where the temperature is more favorable for a young newlywed couple than the hot desert air that scorches the valleys. The fragrance of Solomon's wife provided a cozy, tranquil place where he could enjoy her and be refreshed by her fruits and undisturbed garden.

> [8] *Come with me from Lebanon, my spouse, with me from Lebanon: look from the top of Amana, from the top of Shenir and Hermon, from the lions' dens, from the mountains of the leopards.*
>
> *Song of Solomon 4:8 (KJV)*

> [11] *Thy lips, O my spouse, drop as the honeycomb: honey and milk are under thy tongue; and the smell of thy garments is like the **smell of Lebanon**.*
>
> *Song of Solomon 4:11 (KJV)*

31

The Spiritual Scent Spa Rooms: Getting The Scent Massaged In

Get ready to explore the spiritual fragrance rooms where the Shulammite woman received her anointed fragrances. Although she had her fragrances working together she still had reservations about herself and the way she was treated. She mentions three things in chapter 1:5-6 that she considered disadvantages: 1) Her skin was burned from working in the sun everyday; 2) Her mother's children did not like her; 3) She was economically disadvantaged, being made to work in the vineyards. Even though she had physical, emotional and economical disadvantages she still had a spiritual fragrance that attracted the nose and caught the eye of a king who would pursue her all the way to the altar.

You may feel as though you have some disadvantages (we all do). Tell those negative thoughts and feelings good-bye because I'm going to show you how the Shulammite woman overcame her disadvantages. For example, when faced with being burnt by the sun, she said, "I am black but beautiful". What she meant was, outwardly she may not fit the popular model of beauty, but she possessed an attractive spiritual beauty with gifts and fragrances great enough to please her king.

Each and every one of these Nine Spices will speak to the Nine Spiritual Fruits and Gifts of the wife of Solomon. She was a woman who had given herself wholly to the Lord. He anointed her, gifted her and made her to bring forth much fruit.

The NINE Spiritual Scents

[13] *Thy plants are an orchard of pomegranates, with pleasant fruits;* **1. camphire***, with spikenard,* [14] **2. Spikenard** *and* **3. saffron***;* **4. calamus** *and* **5. cinnamon***, with all trees of* **6. frankincense***;* **7. myrrh** *and* **8. aloes***, with all the* **9. chief spices***:*

Song of Solomon 4:1
(modified to show the nine scents)

The Spiritual Scent Spa Rooms: Getting The Scent Massaged In

The NINE Fruit (Graces) of the Spirit

[22] *But the fruit of the Spirit is **1. love, 2. joy, 3. peace, 4. longsuffering, 5. gentleness, 6. goodness, 7. faith** , [23] **8. meekness, 9. temperance**: against such there is no law.*

Galatians 5:22-23
(modified to show the nine fruit)

The NINE Spiritual Gifts

[7] *But the manifestation of the Spirit is given to every man to profit withal.* [8] *For to one is given by the Spirit the **1. word of wisdom**; to another the **2. word of knowledge** by the same Spirit;* [9] *To another **3. faith** by the same Spirit; to another the **4. gifts of healing** by the same Spirit;* [10] *To another the **5. working of miracles**; to another **6. prophecy**; to another **7. discerning of spirits**; to another **8. divers kinds of tongues**; to another the **9. interpretation of tongues**:* [11] *But all these worketh that one and the selfsame Spirit, dividing to every man severally as he will.*

I Corinthians 12:7-11
(modified to show the nine gifts)

33

The Spiritual Scent Spa Rooms: Getting The Scent Massaged In

Take a look at what the Fragrances, Fruit and Gifts of the Spirit look like side by side in their biblical order. See the chart below.

Fragrance Song of Solomon 4:11	*Fruit* Galatians 5:22-23	*Gifts of the Spirit* I Corinthians 12:7-11
Camphire	Love	Word of Wisdom
Spikenard	Joy	Word of Knowledge
Saffron	Peace	Faith
Calamus	Longsuffering	Gifts of Healing
Cinnamon	Gentleness	Working of Miracles
Frankincense	Goodness	Prophecy
Myrrh	Faith	Discerning of Spirits
Aloes	Meekness	Divers Kinds of Tongues
Chief Spices	Temperance	Interpretation of Tongues

The Spiritual Scent Spa Rooms: Getting The Scent Massaged In

Your Cleansing

Jesus anticipated your arrival. He has so much prepared for you and many things to share as He places His anointed spices into your spirit.

Before I can take you into the spiritual spa rooms I've been given the assignment of first leading you in a prayer of confession. Now, you may read this book and enjoy the contents without repeating the following, but you will not benefit nearly as much. If you truly want to benefit from the full aroma package (Psalm 103:2 and 116:12) then believe in your heart and **sincerely** repeat the following:

> Lord Jesus, I believe you are the Son of God.
> I believe you died and on the third day rose again.
> I confess I am a sinner.
> I believe you died to cleanse me of all of my sins.
> I receive forgiveness for my sins.
> Now Lord Jesus I open my heart and ask you to be the Lord of my life.
> I confess with my mouth that I am forgiven.
> I am saved and I am a child of God. Amen

Now that you have given your life to Christ I recommend you find a church that is firmly rooted in the word of God and believes in the power of Jesus' spirit. Commit yourself to it by attending regularly, supporting it financially and praying for its success.

Secondly my job is to baptize you for cleansing purposes just as John the Baptist did in preparing the people to meet Jesus through the Baptism of Repentance from sin (Mark 1:4-5). This baptism is a cleansing and washing away of old ways and behaviors. It is an outward event that declares you are leaving a life of sin to live a life like Jesus the Son of God.

Being submerged in a body of water is almost like being buried then coming back to life again.

The Spiritual Scent Spa Rooms: Getting The Scent Massaged In

[10] And Elisha sent a messenger unto him, saying, Go and wash in Jordan seven times, and thy flesh shall come again to thee, and thou shalt be clean. [11] But Naaman was wroth, and went away, and said, Behold, I thought, He will surely come out to me, and stand, and call on the name of the LORD his God, and strike his hand over the place, and recover the leper. [12] Are not Abana and Pharpar, rivers of Damascus, better than all the waters of Israel? may I not wash in them, and be clean? So he turned and went away in a rage. [13] And his servants came near, and spake unto him, and said, My father, if the prophet had bid thee do some great thing, wouldest thou not have done it? how much rather then, when he saith to thee, Wash, and be clean? [14] Then went he down, and dipped himself seven times in Jordan, according to the saying of the man of God: and his flesh came again like unto the flesh of a little child, and he was clean.

II Kings 5:10-14 (KJV)

Naaman was a great warrior in the Bible but he had leprosy, a disease associated with sin. If a person had leprosy they were considered unclean and had to live in colonies away from the cities and daily life. He began to look for a remedy for his condition. His servant told him about the prophet Elijah who instructed Naaman to go and dip his entire body in the Jordan River seven times. Seven is the number of completion. Naaman had to baptize himself until he was completely cleansed of sin.

[3] Know ye not, that so many of us as were baptized into Jesus Christ were baptized into his death? [4] Therefore we are buried with him by baptism into death: that like as Christ was raised up from the dead by the glory of the Father, even so we also should walk in newness of life. [5] For if we have been planted together in the likeness of his death, we shall be also in the likeness of his resurrection: [6] Knowing this, that our old man is crucified with him, that the body of sin might be destroyed, that henceforth we should not serve sin. [7] For he that is dead is freed from sin.

The Spiritual Scent Spa Rooms: Getting The Scent Massaged In

[8] Now if we be dead with Christ, we believe that we shall also live with him:

Romans 6:3-8 (KJV)

I am going to walk you through these spiritual spa rooms. Upon your arrival, you will be met by Mr. Marvelous (Psalm 118:23) none other than Jesus Christ the Perfume Maker who is waiting to anoint you with gifts and make you fruitful. He will speak His word into you and baptize you with the Holy Ghost and with fire (Luke 3:16). Let us begin.

#1
The Room of Camphire

Theme colors: White and Yellow

Welcome, in this room you will learn information on developing the power of the camphire fragrance. It is here where Jesus will baptize you in this anointed spiritual scent.

Many changes will occur for your good, so take off those old spiritual shoes for you are standing on Holy Ground (Exodus 3:5). Take off those old worn out garments and allow the angels to clothe you with new garments of Praise, Joy and Humility (Zechariah 3:3-5).

*[3] To appoint unto them that mourn in Zion, to give unto them **beauty** for ashes, the **oil of joy** for mourning, the **garment of praise** for the spirit of heaviness; that they might be called trees of righteousness, the planting of the LORD, that he might be glorified.*

Isaiah 61:3 (KJV)

The Spiritual Scent Spa Rooms: Getting The Scent Massaged In

What is Camphire?

Also known as henna, it produces clusters of small white and yellow aromatic flowers. From its leaves comes the peculiar auburn dye with which women in the east stain the palms of their hands and nails. It is an evergreen leaf plant, which grows six to eight feet high and is mostly used for hedges.

You must travel to the Middle East near Jerusalem to find this anointed and fragrant spice. The exact location is called En-gedi, the only place to find it. Pack your spiritual bags and let us travel in the Spirit of the Lord to this location.

Fragrance

Camphire was the first fragrance Solomon noticed on the Shulammite woman. He mentioned it first because it was her foundational spice. She excited Solomon's emotions and drew him closer with her camphire.

En-gedi is where David sought refuge from Saul (I Samuel 24:1). It was not far from the Dead Sea where nothing could live, yet En-gedi was like a fountain of life. It was an important oasis with fresh water and hot springs, like a natural spa with lots of colorful flowers, including an abundance of the camphire plant (Song of Solomon 1:14).

Jesus is our camphire plant that can only come from one place. Just as En-gedi was a refuge and a hiding place for David, so is Jesus a refuge and hiding place for the believer. Jesus is the true manifestation of camphire the love spice because He said "Greater love hath no man than this, that a man lay down his life for his friends" (John 15:13).

Fruit

Camphire is an anointing of the fruit of Love. It represents the Love of God. Unlike the other fragrances it can only be found in

The Spiritual Scent Spa Rooms: Getting The Scent Massaged In

one source. True love comes from God. Love compelled God the Father to give us His only begotten Son, "For God **so** loved the world that He gave" (John 3:16). You need this fragrance in order to have a foundation for the other spices to be laid upon. You cannot build a life for God without having the Love of Jesus in your heart. Relax as the Lord Jesus pours these words out until they become a part of you.

> *43 Ye have heard that it hath been said, Thou shalt love thy neighbour, and hate thine enemy. 44 But I say unto you, Love your enemies, bless them that curse you, do good to them that hate you, and pray for them which despitefully use you, and persecute you; 45 That ye may be the children of your Father which is in heaven: for he maketh his sun to rise on the evil and on the good, and sendeth rain on the just and on the unjust. 46 For if ye love them which love you, what reward have ye? do not even the publicans the same? 47 And if ye salute your brethren only, what do ye more than others? do not even the publicans so? 48 Be ye therefore perfect, even as your Father which is in heaven is perfect.*
>
> *Matthew 5:43-48 (KJV)*

A God-centered love is what the world needs to see in you, if you are to show them the way to God. Not to mention love is a very attractive characteristic to have. When you get married your husband will need your love. You will come across times in the marriage when he seems to be more of an enemy than a husband, but your job is to keep the love alive.

If you are single you should be showering your love on God. Love keeps you faithful, closer to God in prayer and restrains you from making mistakes and bad decisions that are not pleasing to Him. Love is a keeper. Jesus said, "If you love me, keep my commandments" (John 14:15). The Bible says to love the Lord with all your heart, soul, mind and strength (Mark 12:30). The fruit of love will grow stronger the more you exercise it. ""And now

The Spiritual Scent Spa Rooms: Getting The Scent Massaged In

abideth faith, hope, love, these three; but the greatest of these is love" (I Corinthians 13:13).

Gift of the Spirit

Camphire will cause you to speak words of wisdom to people around you. Your words should be wise and directional towards the Lord. This anointing will cause you to guard your mouth. According to James 3:4-5, your words can guide ships or sink them. The foolish say whatever comes to mind, whether it is good or bad. They say things without regard for other people's feelings and even speak badly concerning their own homes, lives and children. If God has blessed you with the camphire gift, you have His wisdom in your spirit. Speaking the Word of Wisdom will bless your life with godly direction; not only for your future but also for those you know and love. This gift was so important Solomon asked for it when he became king of a nation. God was pleased with his request and not only granted him wisdom, but fame and wealth also.

"[29] And God gave Solomon wisdom and understanding exceeding much, and largeness of heart, even as the sand that is on the sea shore. [30] And Solomon's wisdom excelled the wisdom of all the children of the east country, and all the wisdom of Egypt. [31] For he was wiser than all men; than Ethan the Ezrahite, and Heman, and Chalcol, and Darda, the sons of Mahol: and his fame was in all nations round about. [32] And he spake three thousand proverbs: and his songs were a thousand and five. [33] And he spake of trees, from the cedar tree that is in Lebanon even unto the hyssop that springeth out of the wall: he spake also of beasts, and of fowl, and of creeping things, and of fishes. [34] And there came of all people to hear the wisdom of Solomon, from all kings of the earth, which had heard of his wisdom."

I Kings 4:29-34 (KJV)

The Spiritual Scent Spa Rooms: Getting The Scent Massaged In

Healing Power

As the camphire spice is being massaged in, healing is taking place in your body. It is known to protect against surface bacteria and fungi. It helps to heal small cuts and burns and is used as a mouthwash for bad breath and to heal sore throats. Its healing power is used in internal medicines to treat nervousness and diarrhea and has been known to cure colds, chills and inflammation.

Before entering the next fragrance room, let's see if camphire has absorbed into your spirit.

1. *What is the true spirit of camphire?*

2. *Why was camphire the first fragrance Solomon mentioned?*

3. *What gift is associated with camphire?*

4. *What fruit is associated with camphire?*

5. *What attribute of camphire will keep you?*

6. *Why do you need the Word of Wisdom?*

7. *Finish this statement: You should love the LORD your God with all your _____, _____, _____ and _____.*

8. *List three ailments Camphire heals: _____, _____, _____.*

9. *Finish this statement: God is _____.*

It's time to enter the next anointed fragrance room.

#2
The Room of Spikenard

Theme colors: Rose and Brown

The Spiritual Scent Spa Rooms: Getting The Scent Massaged In

Welcome, in this room you will learn information on developing the power of the spikenard fragrance. It is in this room where Jesus will baptize you in this anointed spiritual scent.

What is Spikenard?

A highly perfumed ointment, spikenard was prepared from a plant in India growing in short spikes. Prized by the ancients, it was very costly, a favorite perfume at baths and banquets.

Fragrance

Spikenard is highly fragrant with an aroma that travels a considerable distance. It was very abundant throughout the east especially in India, yet a high demand drove up its cost. Your spiritual spikenard can reach a greater distance than all the other fragrances. Its attractive aroma makes people want to be a part of what you have going on. It has a beautiful scent, but can be very potent in large amounts. Spikenard should be kept safe and used only for very special reasons. Mary Magdalene broke her alabaster box of spikenard and poured it on the feet of Jesus. She knew there would be no greater occasion and no greater privilege in life than to be at His feet.

Look for a moment at how this fragrance is harvested. When harvested, its roots are the desirable part. You should understand when a plant is taken up by the root that usually results in its demise. When I do yard work around my house I pull up unwanted weeds by the roots so they cannot grow back. That's what evil men desired for Jesus. They wanted to take Him up by the roots (Matthew 21:37-39) and remove all mention and memory of Jesus completely from the earth. Those evil men didn't realize when they killed Him that His fragrance would be given to us (John 16:7-8 and Acts 2:4). Jesus' fragrance of power was not available to us until He was taken up into heaven (Acts 1:11,22). Jesus was the spikenard tree taken up by men attempting to remove His roots and stop all reproduction of His seed. Man's wicked plans end up working for the good of those who are in God's plans. God is still using that spikenard fragrance to anoint us so the memory of Jesus remains in the earth.

> [10] *And in that day there shall be a root of Jesse, which shall stand for an ensign of the people; to it shall the Gentiles seek: and his rest shall be glorious.*
>
> *Isaiah 11:10 (KJV)*

> [31] *And the remnant that is escaped of the house of Judah shall again take root downward, and bear fruit upward:*
> *Isaiah 37:31 (KJV)*

> [5] *And one of the elders saith unto me, Weep not: behold, the Lion of the tribe of Juda, the Root of David, hath prevailed to open the book, and to loose the seven seals thereof.*
>
> *Revelation 5:5 (KJV)*

> [16] *I Jesus have sent mine angel to testify unto you these things in the churches. I am the root and the offspring of David, and the bright and morning star.*
>
> *Revelation 22:16 (KJV)*

Fruit

Joy is an outward expression of an inner connection with God. It does not show itself because of circumstances, whether good or bad. It is the will of God for you to experience joy in this life and the life to come. Spikenard's fruit is abundant joy, unspeakable and full of glory (I Peter 1:8).

> [11] *Thou wilt shew me the path of life: in thy presence is fulness of joy; at thy right hand there are pleasures for evermore.*
>
> *Psalm 16:11 (KJV)*

The Spiritual Scent Spa Rooms: Getting The Scent Massaged In

Joyous people are very attractive because they make you feel as though everything will be all right. Their outlook towards life is contagious, their upbeat energy is electrifying, and their optimistic views are refreshing. A person who bears the fruit of joy can walk into a room, start a conversation with one person and end up with a crowd because people are drawn to their energy. Joy is the fruit that caused Jesus to endure the cross. Joy was set before His eyes and served as His strength (Hebrews 12:2). Joy is your strength as well, while being connected to Jesus and pleasing the heart of God with holy living.

Joy is second only to love, which speaks of its importance to the Christian lifestyle. It is next to impossible to be a true Christian and not have joy. It is a portion of our inheritance. As a matter of fact, Jesus promised us joy.

> [11] *These things have I spoken unto you, that my joy might remain in you, and that your joy might be full.*
>
> *John 15:11 (KJV)*

Gift of the Spirit

The Word of Knowledge is given concerning people, places and/or things as the Holy Spirit directs. It is a gift that helps the lost find their way and reveals divine knowledge about their circumstances. Jesus gave the woman at the well direct knowledge about her past and her current situation.

> [16] *Jesus saith unto her, Go, call thy husband, and come hither.* [17] *The woman answered and said, I have no husband. Jesus said unto her, Thou hast well said, I have no husband:* [18] *For thou hast had five husbands; and he whom thou now hast is not thy husband: in that saidst thou truly.* [19] *The woman saith unto him, Sir, I perceive that thou art a prophet.*
>
> *John 4:16-19 (KJV)*

The Spiritual Scent Spa Rooms: Getting The Scent Massaged In

[7] The lips of the wise disperse knowledge: but the heart of the foolish doeth not so.

Proverbs 15:7 (KJV)

[15] There is gold, and a multitude of rubies: but the lips of knowledge are a precious jewel.

Proverbs 20:15 (KJV)

Healing Power

It is commonly reported that spikenard is used to fight allergies, inflammation, rashes and bad nerves. It can also be used as a deodorant, laxative and sedative for stomach pain.

Before entering the next fragrance room, let's see if spikenard has absorbed into your spirit.

1. *In what country is spikenard found?*

2. *What part of the Spikenard plant produces its fragrance?*

3. *For what occasions was spikenard used?*

4. *What is spikenard's fruit?*

5. *What is spikenard's gift?*

6. *What is an example of a Word of Knowledge?*

7. *What is the purpose of joy?*

8. *Should you have joy in your life?*

9. *List three ailments spikenard heals:* _____, _____, _____.

It's time to enter the next anointed fragrance room.

The Spiritual Scent Spa Rooms: Getting The Scent Massaged In

#3
The Room of Saffron

Theme colors: Yellow and Rose

Welcome, in this room you will learn information on developing the power of the saffron fragrance. It is here where Jesus will baptize you in this anointed spiritual scent.

What is Saffron?

A very rare and luxurious spice found in Palestine. The center portions of its flowers are pressed into saffron cakes, commonly eaten in the Middle East. It is used as a condiment for foods, adding flavor and visual appeal with its rich yellow color. The fragrance is harvested not from the entire flower, but from three threadlike stems in the center. It takes 75,000 of these threads picked by hand to produce one pound of the spice, making it extremely expensive.

Fragrance

Saffron is hard to come by because of the tremendous efforts needed to produce this fragrance. You don't need much of it to have a strong presence. This reminds me of the people who wanted to crucify Jesus. They only desired to end His life. They did not care about His body and left it hanging between two thieves. They didn't know that by taking His life Jesus would leave behind the anointing of the Holy Spirit with His followers. Even the part of the saffron flower not harvested for the fragrance is used to make bread and cakes, and add flavor to food. We should not discard His Body because it serves as a witness to Jesus coming to earth in the flesh. Jesus said, "I am the living bread which came down from heaven" (John 6:51).

Fruit

The priceless fruit of peace is an anointing of the mind and the

46

The Spiritual Scent Spa Rooms: Getting The Scent Massaged In

situation in the wilderness being tempted of the devil, but enduring longsuffering He was relieved and served by the Angels.

> [10] *Then saith Jesus unto him, Get thee hence, Satan: for it is written, Thou shalt worship the Lord thy God, and him only shalt thou serve.* [11] *Then the devil leaveth him, and, behold, angels came and ministered unto him.*
>
> Matthew 4:10-11 (KJV)

Healing Power

Calamus was often used to relieve headaches and reduce lack of mental focus. It also served as an anti-bacterial agent, cured upset stomach, and vertigo.

Before entering the next fragrance room, let's see if calamus has absorbed into your spirit.

1. *What abundant element does calamus grow in?*

2. *What part of the plant is used for fragrance?*

3. *What is calamus' fruit?*

4. *What is calamus' gift?*

5. *Is longsuffering only a human trait? Explain.*

6. *Why is calamus considered a masculine spice?*

7. *If you endure the pain what does longsuffering produce?*

8. *Name three things calamus is known to heal.*

9. *Will you use the calamus anointing?*

It's time to enter the next anointed fragrance room.

The Spiritual Scent Spa Rooms: Getting The Scent Massaged In

#5
The Room of Cinnamon

Theme color: Light Brown

Welcome, in this room you will learn information on developing the power of the cinnamon fragrance. It is here where Jesus will baptize you in this anointed spiritual scent.

What is Cinnamon?

A tree of the Laurel family that grows on the Malabar Coast of India, in Ceylon, and China; when dried and rolled into cylinders the inner rind forms the cinnamon spice we are familiar with. When boiled the fruit and coarser pieces of bark yield fragrant oil. It was one of the principal ingredients in the holy anointing oil (Exodus 30:23), indicating an extensive exchange of commerce between Palestine and the East during ancient times.

Fragrance

Cinnamon is a very popular and common spice in most countries, and is used to season a multitude of foods. It is harvested from the bark of the tree, then rolled up, dried and distributed throughout the world. Jesus is the spiritual manifestation of cinnamon because He makes life sweeter. He turns bitter times into better times and bitter issues into something sweet (Exodus 15:23-25). Cinnamon may be common, but from a spiritual standpoint it is unusual because our enjoyment and pleasure from it comes at great a price. Jesus was the cinnamon tree whose bark (skin) was stripped so the world could enjoy the sweetness of the Lord.

> *O taste and see that the Lord is good: blessed is the man that trusteth in him.*
>
> *Psalm 34:8 (KJV)*

The Spiritual Scent Spa Rooms: Getting The Scent Massaged In

> [19] *And he took bread, and gave thanks, and brake it, and gave unto them, saying, This is my body which is given for you: this do in remembrance of me.* [20] *Likewise also the cup after supper, saying, This cup is the new testament in my blood, which is shed for you.*
>
> *Luke 22:19-20 (KJV)*

Fruit

The spirit of gentleness comes with the cinnamon baptism. Gentleness is not exacting the full amount of justice due. It tends to acknowledge the wrong doings of others yet forgive and encourage the offender to get up and move on. That is exactly what David says about God in the following Psalm:

> *"Thou hast also given me the shield of salvation: and thy right hand hath holden me up, and **thy gentleness hath made me great.**"*
>
> *Psalm 18:35 (KJV)*

Gift of the Spirit

The working of miracles is a powerful demonstration of the power, ability, willingness and existence of the True and Living God. It works signs and wonders, which counteract the plans of Satan that seek to limit our faith in God's ability and even His existence. Jesus turned water into wine, walked on water, raised the dead, fed over five thousand people, and calmed the raging winds and seas. He was a miracle worker and promised we would perform greater miracles (John 14:12 and Mark 16:17-18).

Healing Power

Cinnamon is said to help balance blood sugar levels, lower bad cholesterol and speed up metabolism aiding in weight loss. It has been used for thousands of years for stomach problems, toothaches, kidney problems, colds, detoxifying the body and treating the flu.

The Spiritual Scent Spa Rooms: Getting The Scent Massaged In

Before entering the next fragrance room, let's see if cinnamon has absorbed into your spirit.

1. *Cinnamon is harvested from: a plant, a tree, or a root (circle one)*

2. *Name three sweet treats that contain cinnamon.*

3. *How is the cinnamon tree related to Jesus?*

4. *What is cinnamon's fruit?*

5. *What is the purpose of the working of miracles?*

6. *What is the gift of cinnamon?*

7. *Define gentleness.*

8. *List three of the ailments healed by cinnamon.*

9. *Do you understand the cinnamon spice? (Yes or No)*

It's time to enter the next anointed fragrance room.

#6
The Room of Frankincense

Theme color: White

Welcome, in this room you will learn information on developing the power of the frankincense fragrance. It is here where Jesus will baptize you in this anointed spiritual scent.

What is Frankincense?

Imported from Arabia, it is a fragrant gum resin that exudes large yellowish-brown tears from Boswellia trees, grown in Palestine. During Bible times it was one of the ingredients in the perfume of the sanctuary,

The Spiritual Scent Spa Rooms: Getting The Scent Massaged In

and accompanied the meat offering. When burned it emits a fragrant odor, hence this incense became a symbol of the Divine Name and an emblem of prayer.

Fragrance

This spice was seen as a symbol of divinity. The Three Wise Men brought frankincense, myrrh and gold as an offering to baby Jesus. It was worth more than gold and even now it still holds value as a spice among royalty and those who have great wealth. Frankincense makes the offering worthy of fire. When burned it would make white smoke not to mention the fragrant aroma it produced. White is a metaphoric color for righteousness. The name (Hebrew *lebonah*, Greek *libanos*) means white. It was to be placed on the shewbread table before the presence of God. We are now the shewbread, and God has commanded to have His name placed upon us (Exodus 25:30).

> [5] *And thou shalt take fine flour, and bake twelve cakes thereof: two tenth deals shall be in one cake.* [6] *And thou shalt set them in two rows, six on a row, upon the pure table before the LORD.* [7] *And thou shalt* **put pure frankincense** *upon each row that it may be on the bread for a memorial, even an offering made by fire unto the LORD.*
>
> *Leviticus 24:5-7 (KJV)*

When you wear frankincense you are displaying the anointing of the name of God. Jesus said "In my name they will cast out devils" (Mark 16:17). The name of the Lord is a strong tower, the righteous run to Him and are safe.

Fruit

One of the testimonies of Jesus was His goodness (Acts 10:38). He is also the Good Shepherd (John 10:14). Jesus said there is none good but the Father. If we desire the fruit of goodness we must be connected to the GOOD Source. This fragrance encourages you to

The Spiritual Scent Spa Rooms: Getting The Scent Massaged In

let your light so shine before men that they may see your good works and glorify your Father which is in heaven (Matthew 5:16). As a follower of Christ, goodness should be in your nature, not something you have to work hard to achieve. Genuine goodness is very attractive because it is so rare.

Gift of the Spirit

Once this spice is poured out it causes you to prophesy. The prophetic gift speaks with power, authority and assurance as the effective word of God. In the upper room where the disciples and Mary the mother of Jesus gathered to wait on the baptism in the Holy Spirit, the room must have smelled of Frankincense because after the Spirit fell upon them they began to prophesy.

> [17] *And it shall come to pass in the last days, saith God, I will pour out of my Spirit upon all flesh: and your sons and your daughters shall prophesy, and your young men shall see visions, and your old men shall dream dreams:* [18] *And on my servants and on my handmaidens I will pour out in those days of my Spirit; and they shall prophesy:*
>
> *Acts 2:17-18 (KJV)*

Healing Power

Frankincense was popular among the ancients, used to heal every conceivable ailment known to man. In particular it was used as an anti-depressant, to help with asthma, ulcers, body infections, bronchitis, cancer, herpes, high blood pressure, stress, warts, inflammation, allergies, snake bites, to strengthen teeth or stop tooth pain, broken limbs, and burns.

Before entering the next fragrance room, let's see if frankincense has absorbed into your spirit.

1. *What is frankincense?*

The Spiritual Scent Spa Rooms: Getting The Scent Massaged In

2. *How is it harvested?*

3. *How does its fragrance point to Jesus?*

4. *Name its fruit.*

5. *Name its gift.*

6. *Whose name does frankincense represent?*

7. *What type of gift is prophecy?*

8. *What are some things frankincense is known to heal?*

9. *Do you have the frankincense spice? (Yes or No)*

It's time to enter the next anointed fragrance room.

#7
The Room of Myrrh

Theme color: White

Welcome, in this room you will learn information on developing the power of myrrh. It is here where Jesus will baptize you in this anointed spiritual scent.

What is Myrrh?

The fragrant scent comes from the gummy, sap-like substance that leaks from the myrrh tree. Myrrh trees are found throughout the Middle East but are not at all abundant. First mentioned as a principal ingredient in the holy anointing oil, it formed part of the gifts brought by the wise men from the east, which came to worship baby Jesus. Myrrh was used as a perfume and to embalm the dead. It was a custom of the Jews to give those who were condemned to death by crucifixion "wine mingled with myrrh" to produce insensibility. This drugged wine was probably given to the two malefactors that hung at Jesus' sides, but when the Roman soldiers offered it to Jesus "he received it not" (Mark 15:23).

Fragrance

Myrrh was popular among the wealthy, used to bathe the king's wives for purification (Esther 2:12), and was thrown before the king's chariot, perfuming the atmosphere around him. It was one of the principle spices or compounds in the sacred anointing oil to be used only by the Priest. Mary Magdalene brought this spice to the tomb intending to prepare Jesus' body for burial. However, Jesus did not need the myrrh because He had already risen.

Fruit

We have seen faith work as a gift and now we will also see it operate as a fruit of the Spirit. The fruit is different from the gift because the fruit of faith is given to every believer.

> ³ *For I say, through the grace given unto me, to every man that is among you, not to think of himself more highly than he ought to think; but to think soberly, according as God hath dealt to every man the measure of faith.*
>
> *Romans 12:3 (KJV)*

Every believer needs faith to satisfy the heart of God (Hebrews 11:6). Faith to the believer is like blood in the natural body. When blood is pumped throughout the body it receives nourishment and life, but when the blood ceases to flow the body grows cold and lifeless. So it is in your walk with the Lord. As long as your faith is flowing you remain alive in the Spirit, but when your faith stops spiritual coldness and death sets in.

Gift of the Spirit

Discerning of spirits is a precious gift of the Holy Spirit needed by everyone who desires to guard against schemers, tricksters, liars and

The Spiritual Scent Spa Rooms: Getting The Scent Massaged In

deceivers of all kinds. This gift lets you see what is truth and what is false. Discernment does not look at the outward appearance but instead searches the spirit of a person. We must allow this gift to live in us to destroy every lie and magnify the truth.

> *¹Beloved, believe not every spirit, but try the spirits whether they are of God: because many false prophets are gone out into the world.*
>
> *I John 4:1 (KJV)*

Jesus said His sheep know His voice; therefore if we hear any other voice that doesn't align with His word we can discern the spirit operating in them and rebuke it.

> *² But he that entereth in by the door is the shepherd of the sheep. ³ To him the porter openeth; and the sheep hear his voice: and he calleth his own sheep by name, and leadeth them out. ⁴ And when he putteth forth his own sheep, he goeth before them, and the sheep follow him: for they know his voice. ₅ And a stranger will they not follow, but will flee from him: for they know not the voice of strangers.*
>
> *John 10:2-5 (KJV)*

Healing Power

This spice was used in ancient times to strengthen the immune system and heal the following: menopause, stretch marks, athlete's foot, fungal infections, gingivitis, wounds, diarrhea, ulcers, sore throats, and ringworms.

Before entering the next fragrance room, let's see if myrrh has absorbed into your spirit.

1. *Where does myrrh come from?*

2. *What was myrrh used for?*

The Spiritual Scent Spa Rooms: Getting The Scent Massaged In

3. *What is myrrh's fruit?*

4. *What is myrrh's gift?*

5. *The fruit of faith is pleasing to whom?*

6. *Do you feel you are good judge of character? Is that discernment?*

7. *What does myrrh cure in the body?*

8. *Do you have the myrrh Anointing? (Yes or No)*

It's time to enter the next anointed fragrance room.

#8
The Room of Aloes

Theme colors: Green and White

Welcome, in this room you will learn information on developing the power of aloe. It is here where Jesus will baptize you in this anointed spiritual scent.

What is Aloe?

A fragrant spice derived from aloe trees commonly found in China, Siam, and Northern India, which can grow to 120 feet tall. One of the oldest spices known to man (dating back over 4,000 years ago) and highly fragrant, aloes are of great rarity, extracted directly from the wood. A more common type of aloe, called *aghil* by people in India, is taken from dried leaves on the tree. It was given the name *lignum aquile* and *eagle-wood* by Europeans. The Egyptians used it to embalm their dead. Nicodemus brought aloe to embalm the body of Christ (John 19:39).

The Spiritual Scent Spa Rooms: Getting The Scent Massaged In

Fragrance

The aloe tree itself is significant because the highly sought after spice comes from it. This is interesting because Jesus is the Aloe tree cut down so we could benefit from His broken body. Jesus was raised as the son of a carpenter. Carpenters build things out of wood. He represents the wood used in the Mercy Seat, the Table of Shewbread, the Brazen Altar, the Golden Altar and all the boards used in the Tabernacle (Exodus 25 and 26). He is without a doubt the Fragrant Aloe Tree who emitted a sweet aroma when they cut Him down. When life cuts into you, what do you smell like?

Fruit

Meekness is a fruit of the Spirit that exercises patience, submission and humility, making you more open to the will of God rather than your own desires. Meekness brings elevation. How so? The Bible can answer that question. It says if we humble ourselves to God He will lift us up (James 4:10).

> *10 Humble yourselves therefore under the mighty hand of God, that He may exalt you in due time.*
>
> *I Peter 5:6 (KJV)*

All too often we think humility means being a pushover, but that's the world's view. Meekness, in acknowledging our need for God, makes us strong. The meek shall inherit the earth (Matthew 5:5). Jesus was meek and humble. Moses was said to be the meekest man of his day.

> *9 Rejoice greatly, O daughter of Zion; shout, O daughter of Jerusalem: behold, thy King cometh unto thee: he is just, and having salvation; lowly, and riding upon an ass, and upon a colt the foal of an ass.*
>
> *Zechariah 9:9 (KJV)*

> *3 (Now the man Moses was very meek, above all the men which were upon the face of the earth.)*

The Spiritual Scent Spa Rooms: Getting The Scent Massaged In

Numbers 12:3 (KJV)

Gift of the Spirit

Aloe's gift is divers kinds of tongues. It is important to note Jesus is the Master of words. He is Alpha and Omega, the beginning and the ending (Revelation 1:8). Alpha and Omega are the first and last letters of the Greek alphabet. God is Father of the word of truth and Satan is the father of lies. Truth is the only word that will endure. The Bible says God's Word is forever settled in the heavens. Words cannot exist without letters; therefore He will have the first and the last word.

He is the Master of tongues and languages, demonstrated at the Tower of Babel (Genesis 11:1-9). He even used a donkey to speak a word of rebuke (Numbers 22:28-30). On the Day of Pentecost the Holy Ghost fell upon the disciples and made them speak in tongues (languages) as the Spirit of the Lord gave them utterance (Acts 2:1-8). God will teach you how to manage your tongue, out of which can change entire situations for the good or bad.

Healing Power

Aloes have been found to stimulate the pineal gland and limbic area of the brain. The pineal gland is where the sleep agent melatonin is produced and the limbic area houses emotions; so aloes can help to relieve insomnia and depression. It's also known to aid against urinary tract infections, menstrual problems, skin infections, herpes, skin tumors, bronchitis, dry lips and nervous tension.

Before entering the final fragrance room, let's see if aloe has absorbed into your spirit.

1. *What is aloe?*

2. *Where is the aloe tree commonly found?*

3. *What type of job did Joseph (father of Jesus) have?*

The Spiritual Scent Spa Rooms: Getting The Scent Massaged In

4. *What is aloe's Fruit?*

5. *What is aloe's Gift?*

6. *When was the last time you used gentleness in a situation?*

7. *Is the Spirit of the Lord still giving gifts like divers tongues?*

8. *What sicknesses is aloe known to heal?*

9. *Do you understand the aloe fragrance?*

It's time to enter the last anointed fragrance room.

#9
The Room of Chief Spices

Theme colors: Yellow, Red, Green, Blue and White

Welcome, in this final room you will learn about developing the power of the chief spices. It is here where Jesus will baptize you in this spiritual scent.

What are the Chief Spices?

Highly aromatic substances, of which several are named in Exodus chapter 30, used in the sacred anointing oil and to embalm the dead. King Hezekiah stored them in his treasure house.

Besem (*beh'-sem*) fragrance: spicery
Chief = ro'sh (*roshe*): the head, place, time, rank

Fragrance

This fragrance is the least known of the nine because it is harvested from more than one type of plant making it difficult to focus on a

The Spiritual Scent Spa Rooms: Getting The Scent Massaged In

single source. Chief spices were used in the holy anointing oil, forbidden for use by anyone other than the Priest.

The sun's heat caused the sap or gum to come out of the various plants' leaves, thorns and bark. Here we have a parallel to another three-fold state: body, soul and spirit. Jesus' response to the pressure from men was the same. He healed on the Sabbath day when the law forbade it. He raised the dead back to life while men openly ridiculed Him and when faced with death He opened His mouth and said Father forgive them for they know not what they do. What do you smell like when under pressure?

Fruit

Temperance is to be in command of one's self at all times, in all places and in all circumstances. It is self-control to abstain from things God has forbidden. Much like the spice itself, it is pulled from the other fruits surrounding it.

> [5] *And beside this, giving all diligence, add to your faith virtue; and to virtue knowledge;* [6] *And to knowledge* **temperance***; and to temperance patience; and to patience godliness;* [7] *And to godliness brotherly kindness; and to brotherly kindness charity.* [8] *For if these things be in you, and abound, they make you that ye shall neither be barren nor unfruitful in the knowledge of our Lord Jesus Christ.*

> *II Peter 1:5-8 (KJV)*

Gift of the Spirit

The interpretation of tongues is an inspirational gift, similar to the gift of prophecy. Both gifts allow you to hear from God and then proclaim that particular message to others. However, this gift identifies the Spirit of the Lord speaking through someone with divers tongues and then relays the message to others in their native language so all can understand what God is saying.

The Spiritual Scent Spa Rooms: Getting The Scent Massaged In

Healing Power

The chief spices historically were applied to the skin producing a warming affect to aid in easing the pain of arthritis, fatigue, muscle cramps, stress and depression.

Let's see if the chief spices have been massaged into your spirit.

1. *What are the chief spices?*

2. *Where does it come from?*

3. *What is the chief spices fruit?*

4. *What is its gift?*

5. *Have you ever seen or experienced this gift?*

6. *Name three areas in your life where temperance is needed.*

7. *What type of gift is the interpretation of tongues?*

8. *What ailments were healed by the chief spices?*

9. *Do you have the chief spices anointing?*

We have come to the end of our journey through the nine fragrance rooms. I hope you have received and been filled with each fragrance of the Lord.

Chapter 4

Nine Sweet Spices, Nine Fruit and Nine Gifts

¹³ *Thy plants are an orchard of pomegranates, with pleasant fruits;* **camphire** *, with spikenard,* ¹⁴ **Spikenard** *and* **saffron***;* **calamus** *and* **cinnamon***, with all trees of* **frankincense***;* **myrrh** *and* **aloes***, with all the* **chief spices***:*

Song of Solomon 4:13-14 (KJV)

I don't think it is by coincidence that there are nine sweet smelling fragrances, nine fruits of the Spirit and nine gifts of the Spirit. I believe it is by divine design. Each one (fragrance, fruit and gift) has its own distinct work to accomplish in you and through you, much like the Father, Son and Holy Ghost are one (I John 5:7-8). The Father is the originator of the plan; Jesus was the sacrifice and the Living Word of God; and the Holy Ghost is the helper, guide and revealer of the Father's will.

--------------------------**These Three are One**------------------------

Fragrance – for fellowship with man (Proverbs 27:9; Song of Solomon 4:13-14) and God (Exodus 30:30)

Fruit – to show your good works (Ephesians 2:10)

Gifts – to show God at work through you (Mark 16:17-18)

This three-fold group of nine speaks of the variety of the Spirit. One of the many things I appreciate about the Holy Ghost is the different ways He spices up our lives. He has more than one way to speak to us, lead us, use us, heal us, feed us and motivate us. Think about it. Apples don't just grow to be red nor the same size, but instead are diverse in sizes, shapes and colors. Think of any fruit or vegetable and I can show you the variety

Nine Sweet Spices, Nine Fruit and Nine Gifts

among them. Various types of spiritual warfare exist, for example: shouting at a wall, hitting arrows on the ground, breaking pitchers, clapping hands, dancing, singing etc. We have many types of music, various praises and ways to sing (Psalm, hymns and spiritual songs), the Holy Spirit gives great variety. The world is full of different races, cultures, languages, skin colors and ethnicities. Thankfully God has given each and every one us distinction in the amount of fruit, types of gifts and fragrant scents we have. I believe there is someone just for **you;** who loves the way **you** smell, the gifts **you** have, the way **you** smile, the way **you** praise and pray, the way **you** walk and talk.

The number nine is a very interesting number in the Bible. Like many other biblical numbers it has a double meaning. On one hand nine was used to pronounce the judgment of God upon His enemies, but on the other it was used to pronounce something had completed its time of waiting and was now ready to come forth in blessing. Eli was 98 years old when his eyes went dim (I Samuel 4:15). He was being judged for his lack of parental guidance over the house of God concerning his son's behavior, thus the number nine. The number eight indicated a new thing; God was raising up Samuel the young prophet. To us nine is a number of completeness, fullness, a birthing season, the bearing of fruit and finality. In Genesis 17:11 Abram had to cut his foreskin because his birthing season had come and God did not want his flesh to get the glory for it.

Nine in the Bible is made of three segments much like an expectant mother has three trimesters in her pregnancy. Nine is the number of months a woman carries a baby and then she brings forth her fruit.

Review the chart below to see how God reveals Himself in the Trinity: Father, Son, and Holy Ghost; fragrance, fruit and gifts etc. This illustrates the harmony of three as it relates to the fragrance, fruit and gifts revealing the manifestation of the will of God in your life. Three is the number of God and represents a strong bond that is very hard to break.

> [12] *And if one prevail against him, two shall withstand him;*
> *and a **threefold** cord is not quickly broken.*
>
> *Ecclesiastes 4:12*

Nine Sweet Spices, Nine Fruit and Nine Gifts

In the Kingdom of God THREE equals ONE.
Notice the following:

1	2	3
Fragrance	Fruit	Gifts of the Spirit
Father	Son	Holy Ghost
One Lord	One Faith	One Baptism
Spirit	Water	Blood
Abraham	Isaac	Jacob
Mind	Body	Soul
Heart	Mind	Strength
Operations	Administrations	Diversities of Gifts
God	Lord	Spirit
Sun	Moon	Stars
Omnipresent	Omnipotent	Omniscient
Past	Present	Future
Height	Weight	Depth
Solid	Liquid	Gas
The Holy Place	The Sanctuary	The Court
Air	Land	Sea
Morning	Noon	Night
Love	Hope	Faith
Feast of Passover	Feast of Pentecost	Feast of Tabernacle
Animal Kingdom	Vegetable Kingdom	Mineral Kingdom
Holy	Holy	Holy
Which is	Which was	Which is to come
Bud	Blossom	Bring forth fruit
Fruit	More fruit	Much fruit
Thirty	Sixty	Hundred
Songs	Hymns	Spiritual Songs

Your spiritual scent is at its best when you are anointed with the fragrance, display the fruit of the Spirit and show God working through you with the gifts of the Spirit. You cannot have a spiritual fragrance without the fruit and the gifts. God is not God without the Son and the Holy Ghost. Neither can you have life in your body without your soul and spirit. All three must operate together in order to have a complete and fragrant aroma.

Nine Sweet Spices, Nine Fruit and Nine Gifts

List nine spiritual things about yourself that others see, hear or feel. (Example of feel could be healing, deliverance, etc.):

1.

2.

3.

4.

5.

6.

7.

8.

9.

Give the following list with the fruits of the Spirit to your spiritual mentor. Ask them to circle the ones they see in you.

1. Love

2. Joy

3. Peace

4. Longsuffering

5. Gentleness

6. Goodness

7. Faith

8. Meekness

9. Temperance

Nine Sweet Spices, Nine Fruit and Nine Gifts

When handing the list to your spiritual mentor, have them fill it out right then and there; it should only take a few minutes. If they take it home it gives them too much time to think. A spontaneous response is much more sincere than an overnight one. If you have fruit they should be able to name them within a matter of minutes. Let them know it's ok if they cannot circle all nine but to simply circle the ones they can confirm. This will give you something to work with. If you are newly saved and don't have a mentor or friend in the church focus on the very first fruit, which is love, and develop it according to I Corinthians 13.

Ask a female friend from your church to do the same. Once you get the completed lists from your mentor and friend compare them both and note the similarities, which will confirm your fruit. See if you agree with what they circled. Make a note of the ones that are evident and the ones that were not circled. Study them and ask the Lord for those fruits you are missing.

Chapter 5

The Spiritual Nose

*[7] And the LORD God formed man of the dust of the ground, **and breathed into his nostrils the breath of life;** and man became a living soul.*

Genesis 2:7 (KJV)

Your nose has about 40 million receptor sites. Each one is a hole made in a different shape to accommodate various chemicals. When a molecule goes into one of the sites, it acts as a key that unlocks a nerve to your brain causing it to register the odor. Isn't that amazing? Now if the natural is only a shadow or a very small expression of that which is spiritual (Hebrews 10:1) then our spiritual sense of smell must be unbelievably awesome. If the natural man has 40 million receptor sites for smell then the spiritual man is even more superior and limitless when it comes to smell. One would think 40 million anything in the human body is excessive but I believe that speaks of the importance of smell in both the natural and spirit realms.

I know you're probably asking how can a natural man smell a spiritual perfume. He must be spirit filled and tuned in to the Holy Spirit and you must have on the Holy Perfume. It is important that the man has a spiritual nose so he can smell the true you, which is your spirit. He should be able to savor your lifestyle and love to see God in you. If he doesn't have a spiritual nose he will only desire your physical body while dishonoring your fruit and gifts. Need I say this is not the type of man God has for you. Don't settle for a ZERO when God has a PKO (Proclaimer of Kingdom Operations) set a side for you. Stay in position, by living a life that's pleasing to God.

The Spiritual Nose

It is always disheartening for me to see one of my sisters in Christ settle for an Almost or So-Close man. He was Almost saved and So-Close to the real thing. These women know the man they have settled for is not the one but they have reasoned with themselves, searing their conscience in the process. As a matter of fact he's not truly saved, is he? He probably doesn't know anything about the church because he only attends on special occasions. He most likely doesn't know the simplest thing about the Kingdom of God, sounding out of place when he prays. He may look and act uncomfortable around the saints. Am I right? Let me tell you what Bro. Almost and Deacon So-Close will do once you marry them. You may be facing these exact problems right now:

1. He will not pray at home or at church (he was not doing this in the first place).

2. He begins finding fault with just about everyone and everything in the church.

3. He accuses you of wanting the Pastor.

4. He stops giving to the church.

5. He stops attending church.

6. He does not want you to attend church.

7. He keeps a lot of division going on in your relationship.

8. He becomes unhappy demanding you find another church or stop going altogether.

9. He arranges romantic or family activities when it's time to go to church, forcing you to choose.

10. He becomes abusive (verbally and/or physically).

As you can see, marrying Brother Almost and Deacon So-Close is not worth the investment of time and it is a waste of fragrance. You deserve to have a marriage that will last a lifetime, weather the storms (there will be some) and come through holding hands saying 'we made it'.

The Spiritual Nose

Most single women are just hoping for a bargain man. They are so fed up with waiting they will accept whatever comes their way. One of the most popular businesses of our day is the dollar store. I have learned my lesson about purchasing items from these places. One day I bought a broom from a dollar store. That broom was so soft it hardly swept or even moved the dirt on the floor. I had to work doubly hard to clean a spot that would have taken half the time with a regularly priced, better quality broom. I came to the conclusion the dollar store is not such a bargain after all. It's the same with the bargain men so many sisters keep settling for. It would take three or four of them to complete you like a quality man can. Ain't nothing like the real thing.

You need not have a spiritual perfume unless there is someone besides the Lord who can smell and enjoy it. God created you for man. That is why God blessed you with the natural and spiritual desires to be with him and the capabilities to please him.

You and the man were made for each other spiritually, physically and emotionally. The Bible declares, "the woman was made for the man" (I Corinthians 11:9). Repeat that to yourself. Declare and agree with God's Word.

I Was Made For The Man

Men cannot live out God's original plan without you and you cannot live out God's original plan without the man. We are co-laborers and co-dependants together in God's plan. Don't get me wrong. You can live a happy and satisfying life as a single woman. However, if you don't want to you don't have to, and if you don't have to why should you? Be encouraged. Wear your spiritual fragrance and attract yourself a man after God's own heart.

Stop feeling as though you have sinned or like you are not worthy to be called a child of God because you desire to be married. Instead exercise your faith for a husband. Ask the Lord for more of the perfume that would draw him to you. Stop fearing and don't panic. God has not given us the spirit of fear; but of love, and power and a sound mind (II Timothy 1:7).

The Spiritual Nose

Hear this, it is not wrong to want to be married; it is God's will. Is God's will wrong? No! Every enemy of God is a liar but every word of God is true. God saw the man was lonely and He said it's **not good** for man to be alone. God made you to be a help meet, a partner, and a friend. It is important you realize men who are doing something with their lives are looking for help and comfort in a world of discomfort, i.e. a wife.

When Adam was alone God decided to make him a companion. Out of all the things that God could have made He created a woman. That's how important you are to God and man. God knew you were just what the man needed. Some lonely single man needs (fill in your name) _____ by his side. The name Comforter is used in the same sense as the name Holy Ghost. When you pray and ask in the Name of Jesus to send you a husband, you **are** praying in the will of God knowing He hears you and will grant your prayer request (I John 5:14-15).

> *16 And I will pray the Father, and he shall give you another Comforter, that he may abide with you for ever;*
>
> *John 14:16 (KJV)*

> *26 But the Comforter, which is the Holy Ghost, whom the Father will send in my name, he shall teach you all things, and bring all things to your remembrance, whatsoever I have said unto you.*
>
> *John 14:26 (KJV)*

Comforter in the Greek translates ***parakletos***, meaning literally "one called alongside to help". This is really something to ponder in your heart, woman of God. You were created to be the parakletos, to stand alongside and help the man who will be your husband. You are destined to be the manifested expression of the Holy Ghost to him.

> *And the Lord God said, It is not good that the man should be alone. I will make him an **help meet** for him.*
>
> *Genesis 2:18 (KJV)*

74

The Spiritual Nose

[34] There is difference also between a wife and a virgin. The unmarried woman careth for the things of the Lord, that she may be holy both in body and in spirit: but she that is married careth for the things of the world, how she may please her husband. [35] And this I speak for your own profit; not that I may cast a snare upon you, but for that which is comely, and that you may attend upon the Lord without distraction.

I Corinthians 7:34-35 (KJV)

For far too long churches have made single women feel guilty and less spiritual because they 'had the nerve' to want to be married. In churches where the leadership doesn't bother to minister to single people I often hear the women saying things like "I don't need a man, I'm happy being single". Yet these same women inquire about every single male Evangelist that comes to town. I sometimes hear them say things like "I'm more interested in pleasing God". Most of the time that is a self-protective approach being used to hide their true feelings (they want to be married).

A Harvest of Men

It is time for those who are saved – married or single, to pray to the **Lord of the Harvest** (Matthew 9:38) and ask Him to release a harvest of men into the church. We need a harvest of men who will have a "Yes Lord" on their lips and Jesus in their hearts; who will spend time in the presence of the Lord until His Glory fills them (Exodus 34:34-35). All of us have male family members, close friends, associates and so forth that are bound, under attack and whirling in a violent generational cycle that seems to get worse with every generation and can't get right. We must fast and pray together for their deliverance until every one of Pharaoh's soldiers, prison guards, habits and misleading mindsets are drowned by the power of God.

The lack of men in the church is not just a problem here in the United States but in churches all over the world. The Spirit of the Lord is strongly urging me to alert the church to pray and place a demand on the spiritual freedom of men. We should be declaring enough is enough, and take authority in the Spirit. Only then we will see an overwhelming harvest of

75

The Spiritual Nose

men flowing into the churches worldwide; men who will take their place in the home, in ministry and in the community. I urge you to join my worldwide prayer team for men's deliverance online at www.spiritualfragrance.org

It is time for the church to stop being ashamed of its single members' issues and concerns and stop acting as though prayer and faith will not help. Ask yourself why wouldn't prayer help? Is there anything too hard for the Lord? The time has come for the church to begin boldly declaring the will of God concerning marriage and agree with the singles and with the Word until our churches are overrun with weddings, smiling faces, baby showers and first-time home buyers.

The only way to reap a harvest of any particular kind is for the seed of that fruit to be planted. If you want oranges you cannot plant apple seeds and expect orange trees to spring forth. We will begin to experience a harvest of men in the coming months and years, and no one can stop it. Jesus came to the earth as a man-child (a male seed) and He became the seed that fell into the ground and died so a male harvest would turn their families unto God with sincere hearts, just like the Son of God.

> *24 Verily, verily, I say unto you, Except a corn of wheat fall into the ground and die, it abideth alone: but if it die, it bringeth forth much fruit.*
>
> *John 12:24 (KJV)*

Most of us are familiar with that scripture but do we really know the power behind the fact that Jesus was a human male? I believe Jesus being a male has great significance. It explains why Satan fights men and uses all kinds of tactics to keep men out of the church. The devil is afraid they will grow to be like The Seed (Jesus).

God allowed Jesus to be placed on the cross and laid in a tomb because He knew Jesus alone could reap more by sacrificing himself. He could reap men who would sacrifice their lives for the kingdom, their wives and their children (Ephesians 5:25).

The Spiritual Nose

I live in Northern California in a city called Fairfield where I pastor a young, growing, spirit baptized church (Bountiful Harvest C.O.G.I.C.). Fairfield is about thirty-five minutes from Oakland and around forty-five minutes from San Francisco, depending on traffic. I was sickened in my spirit as I watched the newly appointed San Francisco Mayor Gary Newsome line up homosexual men by the thousands from around the world and gave them approval to get married.

The images were filthy, horrendous and very abominable. Local and world news cameras were on hand to capture the long line of men kissing and caressing each other, smiling, celebrating and exchanging rings. The lesbian women were doing the same with each other. I couldn't believe it. The devil was dangling weddings before the world in a perverse way. Instead of being outraged the world was at odds as people had their typical debates over the same sex issue. Some thought it was good, some were more concerned for the tradition of marriage and a small number were concerned about the children, because same sex marriages will further confuse this generation. Very few were concerned for the establishment of God in Holy Matrimony.

The enemy lined those men up and paraded them before us all. We didn't realize the enemy was boldly declaring he has the heads of our households in his hands. We were more concerned with ensuring gay marriage didn't become legal and recognized in our courts. Some of our leading Pastors were pushing for the Republican Party to declare it would not allow such a thing, but they were wrong. I was upset with other select ministers because they didn't realize there is a bigger fish to fry than trying to get your political party choice into office. Our men were in trouble. The devil was saying, "Look at your men marrying each other". It was and should be viewed by the church as an outright declaration of war for the souls of men.

Let us seek the Lord for this harvest of men. Never before has there been a people who asked God for such a thing as the male harvest. In Jesus' day He prayed first before selecting His twelve disciples who were all men. During Jesus' ministry He fed large crowds of men twice; once was to four thousand men and the other was to five thousand men plus women

77

The Spiritual Nose

and children (Matthew 15:38 and 14:21).

One thing you will notice about Jesus' harvest of men is it always included women and children. We are not asking for a group of men only but we are asking for the true harvest of men with their families. The Promise Keeper's Men's Ministry came close but there was not enough unity between men and women. Let us move heaven until God moves the earth as we pray for the prison doors to swing wide open and for everyone's bands to be loosed (Acts 16:26).

We as a body of baptized believers stood by (without prayer) and watched, saying to ourselves "what a shame". These men are going to waste with demonic spirits pulling them into hell when we have been given power over the devil. In the mean time the church is full of single women suffering from acute loneliness wondering can God do it, can He send them a husband. The answer is yes.

These men are potential husbands for the women of God. The devil said, "Ha! Look at your men. Look at God's plan falling apart. Didn't God say He made them male and female (Genesis 1:27)? Why are they acting like females?" Satan says, "God may have created them that way but they don't have to live that way", so he warps the minds of men to desire each other sexually. Then some women began to turn to each other for comfort and companionship, adding to the downward spiral of God's plan for family, community and church.

God said to the man and the woman to be fruitful and multiply. Satan's plan is to stop pro-creation through homosexual relationships. These relationships work against human existence because life would come to an end if we all lived that type of lifestyle. They are so confused they adopt children (who exist because a man and a woman came together), which is the very thing they are against. They cannot truly love children because children do not come into being as a result of their sexuality. The unclean spirit that seduced them hates children. They only want to adopt children to try and mock the true family (man and wife), the Church and God. The devil's plan will fail and the word of the Lord will endure forever.

78

The Spiritual Nose

The Lord will equip us with spiritual strategies to deliver the men of our day from the devil's sharp, flaming weapons for generations to come. God will deliver us from the hands of the fowler, the destroyer, and from the arrows and fiery darts of the wicked one. Our men will be saved. They will be used of God. They will be faithful husbands and fathers. In Jesus' name, it is so!!

Beards and Butts

The devil loves to bring shame upon men because they are the heads of God's holy institution of marriage. According to I Corinthians 11:7 the man is the image and glory of God. It is for that very reason Satan targets the man in order to pervert, mar or smear the image of God by way of the man (God's image bearer). God created man and gave him authority to have dominion as the Son of God in the earth (representing God) and Satan didn't like it one bit. Since then Satan has sought every opportunity to embarrass man before other men, angels, demons, women, children, and before God his creator.

> *"When David's men came to the land of the Ammonites, 3. the Ammonite nobles said to Hanum their lord, "Do you think David is honoring your father by sending men to you to express sympathy? Hasn't David sent them to you to explore the city and spy it out and overthrow it? 4. So Hamun seized David's men, shaved off half of each man's **beard**, cut off their garments in the middle at the **buttocks**, and sent them away. When David was told about this, he sent messengers to meet the men, for they were greatly humiliated. The king said, "Stay at Jericho till your beards have grown, and them come back. When the Ammonites realized that they had become a stench in David's nostrils, they hired twenty thousand Aramean foot soldiers from Beth Rehob and Zobah, as well as the King of Maacah with a thousand men, and also twelve thousand men from Tob.*
>
> *II Samuel 10:2-6 (New Living Translation)*

The Spiritual Nose

In the Hebrew culture it was customary for men to wear a full beard. The full beard was a sign of a very mature man and the pride of being a man. The beard also meant authority and male beauty. Their enemies brought shame on them by cutting the backs out of their garments so that their behinds would be exposed to each other and anyone else around. This sounds a lot like the men of our day. Most of the men of our day are immature (having the beard half shaved) and expose their behinds to everyone (garments cut) wearing their pants around their thighs. Let it be noted these were David's men. David is an Old Testament shadow of Jesus Christ. It is safe to say Satan is out to cause shame and embarrassment to Jesus' men.

We must stand up in the Spirit of the Lord and pull down the strongholds, walls and dams holding back the **harvest of men**. Unite with me and the worldwide prayer group. As prayer warriors and intercessors we will bind and cast out the unclean spirits and generational curses from our sons, brothers, uncles, fathers, friends, co-workers and future husbands: www.spiritualfragrance.org.

During the infancy of the church when the leaders (men) were under attack, the Bible said "but prayer was **made** without ceasing of the church unto God" (Acts 12:5). We must **make** prayer for our men. They are being killed, locked up and prepared for the slaughter. If the church doesn't pray, they are in danger of being completely wiped out.

> [1] *Now about that time Herod the king stretched forth his hands to vex* <u>certain</u> *of the church.* [2] *And he killed James the brother of John with the sword.* [3] *And because he saw it pleased the Jews, he proceeded further to take Peter also. (Then were the days of unleavened bread.)* [4] *And when he had apprehended him, he put him in prison, and delivered him to four quaternions of soldiers to keep him; intending after Easter to bring him forth to the people.* [5] *Peter therefore was kept in prison; but prayer was made without ceasing of the church unto God for him.*
>
> *Acts 12:1-5 (KJV)*

The Spiritual Nose

The streets, prisons, war fields, spiritual lion's dens and graves are full of our men and it is up to the church to bring the salvation of the Lord unto them. The church is the only thing on earth that can help this crisis.

He That Findeth A Wife

The man that's coming to find you will be a man with a spiritual nose, a man of love and compassion. He is not looking for a woman who will fall for a one-night fling but he wants a woman with a moral standard, a wife. Good men are looking for women who are living as wives even though they are not married yet, but "he that findeth a *wife* finds a good thing" (Proverbs 18:22). When he finds you will he find a wife or a woman who wants to be married? Practice being a wife. A wife, you ask? Yes. The man is not looking to find you and form you into a wife but instead he wants to find a woman who is walking in the aroma of a wife already. He will be thirsty for life and hungry for fruit. This happened to Jesus when from a distance He saw a fig tree with lots of leaves (the leaves advertised there was fruit on the tree). He went out of His way to go up to the tree to eat of its fruit. When He got close enough to see there was no fruit He cursed it and said "No man eat fruit of thee hereafter for ever" (Mark 11:12-14,20-21). It is refreshing and rare for a man that is looking for a wife to find a woman who is genuine in the faith of Jesus Christ, who advertises what she is, and is actually living what she advertises.

They Could Smell Deborah

People came from all over Israel to see and hear from Deborah. The aroma of God was all over this gifted woman of God. She was married to an awesome man of God named Lapidoth. The name Deborah meant "honeybee" while her husband's name Lapidoth meant "torch". Yes, Deborah was married because her husband had a torch of spiritual light from God and she was like a Honeybee laden with pollen from the fragrant flowers. Lapidoth had a light to show him the way, and Deborah's fragrance was easy to find (Judges 4:4-5).

As a prophetess, Deborah had the fragrance of prophecy and wisdom flowing from her. She was also anointed to be a judge over Israel (Judges 4:4). What is your fragrance? What are your spiritual gifts? What

The Spiritual Nose

torchbearer will be drawn to you?

Adam without God's breath in his nostrils is symbolic of a man without salvation, a man without a nose, a man who cannot smell life. If he can't smell then he won't appreciate your Spiritual Fragrance. Your physical body most likely is the only thing he can understand because it's physical just as he is. He may seem to be alive because he walks, talks and breathes but he is dead while he yet lives because God has not breathed into his nostrils. Jesus told Nicodemus "Truly you must be born again, you cannot see the Kingdom of God" (John 3:3). The breath God gave Adam (mankind) was stolen in the day that he sinned against God's command not to eat the forbidden fruit, saying to him "For in the day that you eat it you will surely die" (Genesis 2:17). Adam and Eve died that day, yet physically they were still alive.

I often wonder how a man can have a good-looking woman who loves him and is willing to do **anything** for him and he never expresses true feelings for her. She can cry for days and nights from her emotional wounds and he doesn't feel it. He can cheat on her with her best friend or sister and never feel guilt or shame but rather be proud of it. He can call her names and talk bad about her to any and everyone and never blink an eye. He can have sex with her and never have feelings for her. He can walk away from her on any given day and not feel the pain of being disconnected from her. How can he beat her black and blue and never say I'm sorry and change his behavior?

Why does your man act this way? The answer is simple. He is not alive; he is a dead man. Let me ask you a question. Do you have a dead man or a living one? Are you sleeping with the dead? Are you trying to get a dead man to marry you? He might agree to marry you but keeps changing the date or gets upset when you talk about marriage. Listen very closely. What would you do if you figured out love you enough to marry you? He is doing just enough to sample that fragrance night after night but you are wasting your fragrance on the dead. What would you do? Would you pack your things and leave or would you continue the deception by telling yourself that he loves you?

The Spiritual Nose

Jesus came to a certain seashore where He encountered a man who had thousands of unclean spirits in him and he lived among the tombs. He lived with the dead. No one could help this man. They tried everything and nothing helped. They could not free him from the grip of those devils. Their every attempt at freeing him and getting him away from the graveyard was unsuccessful.

Some women have tried to undo strongholds in men who live among the tombs by sleeping with them, thinking they could tame him with sex. Some women think they can control a man from the tombs by becoming pregnant with his baby(ies), but he is a man who lives among the dead and he himself is dead. He loves the dark, cold and hollowness of the tombs. Not only that but loves what is in the tombs, the dead. **You** do not have the power to give spiritual life. You can only lead him to the One (Jesus) who has the POWER to raise him up from the dead. Stop trying to be a god with your body; you are only setting yourself up for a downfall.

> *[1] And they came over unto the other side of the sea, into the country of the Gadarenes. [2] And when he was come out of the ship, immediately there met him out of the tombs a man with an unclean spirit, [3] Who had his dwelling among the tombs; and no man could bind him, no, not with chains: [4] Because that he had been often bound with fetters and chains, and the chains had been plucked asunder by him, and the fetters broken in pieces: neither could any man tame him. [5] And always, night and day, he was in the mountains, and in the tombs, crying, and cutting himself with stones.*
>
> *Mark 5:1-5 (KJV)*

The Sampler

A sampler is one who eats the variety platter or sampler dish but is afraid to commit to the entrée or the main meal. Yet there are some who have committed to the entrée and are still sampling (married but have someone else on the side). The sampler is not really interested in the main course because he is so excited about the menu. He can't make up his mind on

The Spiritual Nose

what to commit to, so he samples. They are afraid if they commit to the entrée they are going to be cheated out of having other things on the menu, thinking something else could be better. Some are trying to live a double and even triple life, having four or five women, some with children. These are the samplers.

One who has the spirit of a sampler will pretend to commit to an entrée, but they never do. They pretend to want to marry you by getting engaged. They look over the menu of main courses and continue to tell the waiter they need more time to decide, but when it is time to make a decision and commit they always select the sampler dish. The sampler dish if full of easy women who don't require a commitment. By the time they finish the sampler dish they are full so they send the entrée menu back saying, 'I don't want it, I'm satisfied now'.

Most single women face this same problem today. They can't get their man to commit because he is a sampler. Samplers are everywhere, even inside the church; in your choir stands and pulpits and every place where unknowledgeable women are willing to be sampled. Women who don't require a commitment hurt the ones that do. If he can't get over on a woman because she requires a commitment, then he will simply move on to another woman with lower standards. Ultimately he won't need to return to the woman who requires marriage before intimacy.

Let me give you this little scenario. Do you think a clothing store will put up with a sampler's behavior? I don't think so. Let's say a sampler sees a pair of Nikes, Timberlands or Phat Farm outfits and purchases them. He then takes those clothes home and wears them out to parties or plays basketball in them and to his friend's house or whatever. The sampler then goes back to the store and returns those used and worn clothes and gets his money back knowing he never really planned to keep them. He feels like he is in a game and he is winning. The sampler then goes back to the same store and starts the whole process all over again. I tell you this, by the third or fourth time he takes those clothes and returns them, the store manager will run him off, call security and the police, telling him not to ever come back.

The Spiritual Nose

Some women will allow the sampler to move in and even have children by him, but never get a commitment. He's just sampling their fragrance, eventually he will get enough of it and move on to sample a new spice. Sometimes they might agree to marriage, but just like the man who returns the clothes to the store, he keeps pushing the date back. He never planned to keep the clothes and he never really planned to marry you.

Here is my advice: kick the sampler out of your house and out of your life. Stop wasting your youth, time and fragrance on him before you are four babies deep, twenty-five pounds overweight and twelve years in love; but never married. By then you won't have a fragrance because you lack godly morals and now your personal aroma stinks. Are you looking for a living man or a dead one? If you want a living man then you must put on the spiritual fragrance, fruit and gifts. If he doesn't have the breath of God he cannot smell; and if he can't smell, he can't feel.

Smell is connected to the part of the brain that is called the limbic system where human memory and emotions come from. In my research I found people who suffer from smelling disorders are more likely to become suicidal because they feel as though they are missing out on life even though they are alive. Most (not all) people with smelling disorders have very low self-esteem, mostly because they are unsure of themselves. They can't taste a wonderful meal or smell if their breath is fresh or not. They are unsure around others because they can't smell life. Life is emotional and when a person can't smell, their emotions can be unbalanced as well. People with smelling disorders would truly benefit from your prayers. The same is true in the spirit. If a man can't smell he is more likely to be emotionally out of control.

When a man can smell (having life from God) he is more likely to be emotionally stable. This is backed by the following statistics: people who pray get into less trouble, recover faster from surgery or tragedy, are more likely to get married and stay married, and live longer. Simply put, a man who cannot smell is never satisfied and never will be. Jesus told Nicodemus unless you are born again (regenerated) or unless you are given the breath that comes from God, you cannot see or experience the Kingdom of God. Women that are anointed by Jesus are connected to the

The Spiritual Nose

Kingdom of God. Unless the man you want is born again he can't see, hear or smell the real you.

Chapter 6

Dead Men's Bones

*I*f you are single and saved don't allow any more dead men to put their bones on you. Or should I say do not let another man put unholy bones in your closet. Who are the dead? They are people dead in trespasses and sins (Ephesians 2:1). You cannot afford to lay up with another set of bones at this time in your life. The God you serve has more in store for you. Awake! Arise and listen to the instructions of a **Father** (Proverbs 1:8 and 4:1).

I have seen some heartbreaking cycles cling to single parent homes. For example, a great-grandmother who never married had children by different fathers that were physically abusive, then her daughter fell into the same trap. Unfortunately the cycle gets worse with each generation. We gladly accept the baby and forgive the daughter, yet we fail to reprimand her for getting pregnant in the act of fornication. That does two things: it leaves room for the cycle to continue and the spirit behind the act is never bound then cast out.

You need a spirit inside that continually says "This will not befall me or my children; all curses and evil cycles end now because I am a child of God and I am blessed. No more bones on me. I want them out of my life forever". You have to get the skeletons out and keep them out because living men don't want to be with the dead; especially if they remind him that another man has been in his wife's closet. In other words, if you truly want a husband you will do some spiritual spring-cleaning. Don't allow the bones to condemn you any longer. Their voices must be silenced today. Recommit your life to Jesus and allow the Word of God to speak to you.

Dead Men's Bones

> There is therefore **now** no condemnation to them that are **in** Christ Jesus who walk not after the flesh but after the Spirit.
>
> Romans 8:1 (KJV)

Dead men feed on death and easy situations. If they do not seek life from God they will remain dead and never leave the valley of dry bones. They need to be in a place where they can hear the Word of God to develop their faith (faith comes by hearing and hearing the Word of God).

> [14] But how can they call on him to save them unless they believe in him? And how can they believe in him if they have never heard about him? And how can they hear about him unless someone tells them? [15] And how will anyone go and tell them without being sent?
>
> Romans 10:14-15 (New Living Translation)

If he never wants to go to church, prayer, bible study or any other thing concerning faith in Jesus then you know he is a dead man. My advice to you is to not put stock in dead things because you will lose your investment. Don't waste time, emotions, money, hopes, dreams, trust and love on a corpse.

> The LORD took hold of me, and I was carried away by the Spirit of the LORD to a valley filled with bones. [2] He led me around among the old, dry bones that covered the valley floor. They were scattered everywhere across the ground. [3] Then he asked me, "Son of man, can these bones become living people again?" "O Sovereign LORD," I replied, "you alone know the answer to that." [4] Then he said to me, "Speak to these bones and say, 'Dry bones, listen to the word of the LORD! [5] This is what the Sovereign LORD says: Look! I am going to breathe into you and make you live again! [6] I will put flesh and muscles on you and cover you with skin. I will put breath into you, and you will come

Dead Men's Bones

to life. Then you will know that I am the LORD.' " [7] So I spoke these words, just as he told me. Suddenly as I spoke, there was a rattling noise all across the valley. The bones of each body came together and attached themselves as they had been before. [8] Then as I watched, muscles and flesh formed over the bones. Then skin formed to cover their bodies, but they still had no breath in them. [9] Then he said to me, "Speak to the winds and say: 'this is what the Sovereign LORD says: Come, O breath, from the four winds! Breathe into these dead bodies so that they may live again.' " [10] So I spoke as he commanded me, and the wind entered the bodies, and they began to breathe. They all came to life and stood up on their feet—a great army of them.

Ezekiel 37:1-10 (New Living Translation)

In the natural a woman has a keener sense of smell than a man, especially during pregnancy. Women seem to be more in tune to the environment and their surroundings, maybe because as mothers-to-be they must be aware of danger in the area for the safety of their child. Men on the other hand are not as keen to smell in the natural sense because our focus is much different. We tend to be deeply involved in whatever task is before us, which is why most men are not as good with multitasking.

I remember when my wife became pregnant with our first child. We were both very young, I was 20 and she was 18 when we married. I was a junior at Arizona State University in Tempe (where I majored in Sociology and was a star football player). We were living on my athletic scholarship and my wife's part-time job. We lived in a one-bedroom apartment above a very nice Chinese family and beside a quiet couple from India. Both of these families used a lot of garlic and onions in their cooking but when my wife became pregnant the smell of garlic and onions made her sick. One of the weirdest things happened to me, I began to crave a certain food. Can you guess what it was? Yes you guessed it, onions in the form of onion rings. I wanted homemade onion rings. I had to have them. I made the batter, cut the onions then fried them in the deep

Dead Men's Bones

fryer; but it made her super sick. She banned me from cooking onion rings in the apartment and I agreed.

One day it came time for her regular checkup but I decided to stay home and get some rest. My real agenda was to cook some onion rings. When I finished cooking I threw away the grease, opened all the windows, bleached the counter tops, opened the front door, turned on the fan and had it blowing outward. I also sprayed air freshener and put down some carpet fresh. After all that I sat down and started to play my video game. Home free, right? Think again. About two hours later she came home and immediately smelling the onion rings became sick running to the bathroom hurling up her lunch. I only did it one more time after that. Boy! How she hated me during those onion ring days. One of the funniest things about the whole onion ordeal was a year later after our daughter was born she would go into the kitchen and open a bag of raw onions and eat them like it was an apple.

When God breathes His Spirit into a man he becomes connected to God and he now craves spiritual things. He will literally smell his way to his wife. The Bible says, "He who finds a wife finds a good thing and receives favor from the Lord" (Proverbs 18:22).

In the case of a man searching for a wife he uses all his senses, but the one he depends on the most is his spiritual sense of smell. Smell does not need to hear your voice, see your face, know your skin color or your name. A living man doesn't want to be with anything dead. Living men bury their dead. Living men are attracted to life. One thing about the spiritual sense of smell is it's not limited to being in the area where the smell is. Unlike your man-made perfume, when you are a woman truly anointed by God with His spiritual fragrance it will radiate throughout the earth.

The spiritual fragrance is so powerful it blesses you in all three realms. The first is the natural or earth realm where you are anointed for relationships and bringing souls into the kingdom of God. The second is the universal or spiritual realm to show the wisdom of God defeating the works of the devil. The final realm is the Throne of God, for access to His presence and worship.

Dead Men's Bones

Perfume the Earth

Man was made from the earth; he is earthly. Being an earthly man he is limited to time and space. If he is in New York and wants to travel to California he must have a means of transportation. Even then he can only be in one place at a time. However if he is a man with a nose (a spiritual man) searching for a wife he can be in New York and if there is a woman with a spiritual fragrance in California, he will smell her because spiritual fragrance travels in the spirit (it is not limited). Spiritual Fragrance travels so far that when Jesus was offered up from the earth God the Father smelled Jesus' pleasing aroma all the way in the third heaven, the Throne of God. Prophetic smell is not limited to time and distance and neither is your spiritual aroma; it can be smelled anywhere on earth. How is that possible? The answer is possibilities and abilities are infinite through the power of the Spirit "For with God all things are possible" (Mark 10:27), "For the Spirit also helpeth us in our infirmities" (inabilities and limitations) (Romans 8:26). Prophetic smell will lead him to where you are. He may have an unction, a dream, a vision, a reason to visit, an urge by the spirit to travel or move to your location. He may find you at church, meet you at a job fair, the grocery store or a Christian conference, but he will find you because of your aroma.

Our sense of smell urges us to respond to whatever is giving off the aroma. When a man wants to find where that particular spiritual fragrance is coming from he must come to you. That beautiful, spiritual, heavenly scent Jesus placed on you will bring a spiritual man who will enjoy every sweet spice you have. He will take pleasure in every piece of your delicious fruit and be blessed by the gifts operating in you.

Perfume the Universe

The perfume of Jesus on your life goes into the universe to confound the wisdom of Satan and his fallen host.

> [10] *To the intent that now unto the principalities and powers in heavenly places might be known by the church the manifold wisdom of God,* [11] *According to the eternal purpose which he purposed in Christ Jesus our Lord:*

Dead Men's Bones

Ephesians 3:10-11 (KJV)

When you have been anointed with Jesus' perfume all spiritual beings in the universe know who you are. They can smell the fragrance of the LORD on you. The Bible says He created all things and without Him there was not any thing made (John 1:3).

Fragrances and perfumes can be toxic if over used. Any amount of the Lord's Fragrance is too much for the enemy. Use your fragrance as a weapon against the devil. Ask Jesus the Apothecary (perfume maker) to anoint you with more of His heavenly fragrance to make your enemies choke on the aroma of the Lord. Let it radiate through the godly life you live, the gracious words of your mouth, your prayers and treatment of others.

> *[27] But I say unto you which hear, Love your enemies, do good to them which hate you, [28] Bless them that curse you, and pray for them which despitefully use you.*

Luke 6:27-28 (KJV)

God desires to show you off in the spirit realm (Ephesians 3:10). When you allow God to anoint you, you become known by name to the fallen angels. Your fragrance is so powerful that whatsoever you bind on earth is bound in heaven and whatsoever you loose here is loosed in heaven (Matthew 16:19). Evil spirits must obey the authority of Jesus in you. His Spirit lives in you and they can smell it in the heavens. Remember Jesus has given you power (Luke 10:19). Unclean spirits know who is truly anointed.

> *[13] Then certain of the vagabond Jews, exorcists, took upon them to call over them which had evil spirits the name of the Lord Jesus, saying, We adjure you by Jesus whom Paul preacheth. [14] And there were seven sons of one Sceva, a Jew, and chief of the priests, which did so. [15] And the evil spirit answered and said, Jesus I know, and Paul I know; but who are ye? [16] And the man in whom the evil spirit was leapt on them, and overcame them, and prevailed against*

Dead Men's Bones

them, so that they fled out of that house naked and wounded.

Acts 19:13-16 (KJV)

The perfume of the Lord is only for believers. It is a forbidden fragrance to the world but we can wear it daily (Exodus 30:30-33).

Perfume God's Throne

³⁴ And the Lord said unto Moses, Take unto thee sweet spices, stacte, and onycha, galbanum; these sweet spices with pure frankincense: of each shall there be a like weight: ³⁵ And thou shalt make it a perfume, a confection after the art of the apothecary, tempered together, pure and holy: ³⁶ And thou shalt beat some of it very small, and put of it before the Testimony in the tabernacle of the congregation, where I will meet with thee: it shall be unto you most holy,

Exodus 30:34-36 (KJV)

Another word for perfume is smoke. It is obvious from the verse above God designed a perfumed incense for the priest to burn before the Ark of the Covenant or the Testimony (Holy of Holies).

We must have the aroma of the Apothecary, Jesus the Perfume Maker, to come before the Lord (Exodus 30:25 and 37:29). We must remember it's not us God wants to smell. He wants to smell His Son on us. Not only is Jesus the Perfume Maker but He is also the Perfume. Jesus represents the three sweet spices mentioned above. No part of Jesus is out of balance. He is the sweet spice of stacte (body), onycha (soul) and galbanum (spirit). He wasn't more man than God and He wasn't more God than man. He is equally sweet and fragrant; whether revealing His God side or His man side; He is the perfect God-Man. God desires the same balance for you: to have the same love for Him, the same prayer life and the same commitment. When the pressure is on and the heat is turned up will you remain balanced? Men love a woman who can remain balanced even when all hell is breaking loose. Even when life is beating you up God

93

Dead Men's Bones

desires a sweet balance from the perfume on your life as you represent Him in the earth.

God testified of His Son Jesus Christ the Anointed One over and over again throughout the Bible to prove Jesus would take away sins by pleasing the heart of God through a sin free life. Jesus was the right candidate for the press, the beating and finally death. That's exactly what plants, trees and flowers go through in order to become perfume. They are beaten, pressed, cut down, shuffled, liquefied and minced before they can be worn as a fragrance.

> *[21] Now when all the people were baptized, it came to pass, that Jesus also being baptized, and praying, the heaven was opened, [22] And the Holy Ghost descended in a bodily shape like a dove upon him, and a voice came from heaven, which said, Thou art my beloved Son; in thee I am well pleased.*
>
> *Luke 3:21-22 (KJV)*

Life in the Nose

Ap' is the Hebrew word for nose or nostril. Simply put, it is where man's spirit and body merge enabling him to connect with both the spiritual and earthly realms through the nostril (soul). God blew His Spirit *pneúma* (wind, breath, life, Spirit) into Adam through the nose. It is said the eyes are the windows to the soul, which is true but the nose is where the soul entered. When God breathed into Adam's nose his eyes opened and looked at the physical world. As I have mentioned earlier the nose and sense of smell is connected to the limbic system in the brain where memory and emotions are located. Adam received life through his nose so he could feel, laugh, cry, think and remember. This is very important for you to know. If you meet a man who is disconnected from his emotions it should be a warning signal that he has some physiological issues, needs deliverance or has no life. Do not get involved with these kinds of men. They can be killers, abusers, cheaters and much more. If you want to know if someone is really angry, watch their nose. Anger accelerates the heart, which increases one's breathing pattern thereby causing the nostrils

Dead Men's Bones

to flare open.

When a man with a nose smells your spiritual scent he becomes emotional and gets a burst of energy because of what he smells in the air. He will not forget your scent.

Men love to smell the right perfume on a woman. Your perfume speaks volumes about your personality, sexuality, tastes and energy. Some perfumes can cause men to view you as youthful and energetic, happy and outgoing, friendly and graceful or old and settled in your ways, sad and unhappy, or mean and evil. Wearing the right perfume has its benefits. Your physical perfume is one thing but your spiritual fragrance is what you really want to enhance because it will attract the right man to you.

Men also like to smell the sweet spiritual charisma that flows from a woman who has a connection with God. When a woman is truly connected to God the man feels safe in assuming her body has been kept; not messed over, defiled, and used for another man's pleasure. The man's heart is in close relation to his private parts. The woman covers his heart (an act of trust). God instructed Abraham to circumcise his heart or the foreskin of his flesh (Genesis 17:10-11). The Apostle Paul said the spiritual meaning of circumcision is that of the heart.

> *But he is a Jew, which is one inwardly; and circumcision is that of the heart, in the spirit, and not in the letter; whose praise is not of men, but of God.*
>
> *Romans 2:29 (KJV)*

If he gives you his heart in marriage he must be able to trust you. No man wants to invest his trust then sacrifice all that he takes pride in on something that will not last.

Marriage from a Man's Point of View

Men who refuse to marry typically use the excuse that marriage is only a sheet of paper. If he truly loved and respected you he would go and get the

Dead Men's Bones

paper; after all money is paper, a degree is paper, a car registration is paper, a lease for an apartment is paper, a birth certificate is on paper and a death certificate is on paper. Marriage to most men is the ultimate sacrifice. It is almost like giving up his rights to manhood, like a professional athlete retiring in his prime from a sport he loves. He will not give that away to just any woman. A woman's chastity and sanctified spirit excites a man because men are very territorial. A man wants to know that what he is getting cannot be bought, seduced or romanced away by another man attempting to invade his territory. When a man sees you have been walking the walk and talking the talk he feels you will be true to his love and be his only. It is easier to get a commitment from him by standing your ground on your convictions.

If you do something against your convictions in God then repent and apologize for it later, that's not trustworthy. You will lose his respect and spoil your fragrance at the same time. As a woman with a spiritual fragrance you should not defile yourself. If you stand and let your fragrance flow from holy behavior you will get the best of love in life. If you're going to be a woman with a real fragrance then you've got to be **the real thing**, a woman of spirit and truth (John 4:23-24). God is looking for such to worship Him and real men are looking for this type of woman to marry. Men respect a woman who remains true to her beliefs.

Proverbs 31 paints a picture of an ideal wife:

> [10]*Who can find a virtuous woman? For her price is far above rubies.*
>
> [11]*The heart of her husband doth safely trust in her, so that he shall have no need of spoil.*
>
> [12]*She will do him good and not evil all the days of her life.*
>
> [13]*She seeketh wool, and flax, and worketh willingly with her hands.*
>
> [14]*She is like the merchant's ships; she bringeth her food from afar.*
>
> [15]*She riseth also while it is yet night, and giveth meat to*

Dead Men's Bones

her household, and a portion to her maidens.

[16] She considereth a field, and buyeth it: with the fruit of her hands she planteth a vineyard.

[17] She girdeth her loins with strength, and strengtheneth her arms.

[18] She perceiveth that her merchandise is good: her candle goeth not out by night.

[19] She layeth her hands to the spindle, and her hands hold the distaff.

[20] She stretcheth out her hand to the poor; yea, she reacheth forth her hands to the needy.

[21] She is not afraid of the snow for her household: for all her household are clothed with scarlet.

[22] She maketh herself coverings of tapestry; her clothing is silk and purple.

[23] Her husband is know in the gates, when he sitteth among the elders of the land.

[24] She maketh fine linen, and selleth it; and delivereth girdles unto the merchant.

[25] Strength and honour are her clothing; and she shall rejoice in time to come.

[26] She openeth her mouth with wisdom; and in her tongue is the law of kindness.

[27] She looketh well to the ways of her household, and eateth not the bread of idleness.

[28] Her children arise up, and call her blessed; her husband also, and he praiseth her.

[29] Many daughters have done virtuously, but thou excellest them all.

[30] Favour is deceitful, and beauty is vain: but a woman that feareth the LORD, she shall be praised.

[31] Give her of the fruit of her hands; and let her own works

Dead Men's Bones

praise her in the gates.

Proverbs 31:10-31 (KJV)

DECLARATION

Say these words in faith and agree with God's Word

Father, in the name of Jesus I declare
I am saved and forgiven of all of my sins
through the blood of Jesus.
I am a child of God and I have the breath of God in me.
I agree with your word that I was made for the man and
man will find me because he has your breath in his nostrils.
I am anointed with your spiritual and heavenly fragrance.
I thank you for the institution and gift of marriage because
you have made me a wife.

This I declare in Jesus' name. Amen

Chapter 7

The Human Scent Attraction

*T*he human body produces a hormone called pheromone. These are not detected by the human eye but are easily sensed by the human nose. Pheromones are aromatic chemical compounds produced by one individual that affect the emotions and hormones of another. ***Pherein*** is a Greek word that means to carry, to excite. Studies have shown pheromones are responsible for causing one woman's menstrual cycle to move into the same pattern as another. The study revealed women who worked or lived together for a period of up to four months often began to ovulate at the same time because of the pheromones being released from their sweat glands.

Most people are attracted to fragrances, which is why perfume makers are bringing in billions of dollars every year. Celebrities have jumped into the business by putting their names on fragrances because of the huge market for body oils, powders, lotions, perfumes and the like.

Colognes and perfumes smell differently because individual scent preferences are distinct and gender specific. People wear a particular fragrance because they like the scent and want others to enjoy it as well. I have noticed a woman can wear perfume and not take offence when other women ask about the fragrance or compliment her on it. Men love to smell the right perfume on a woman. The perfect fragrance seems to match your features, skin color, age, energy and so forth. You don't need to spend a long time in his presence either. One hint of a striking perfume will make a man look twice.

Smell triggers our memories. For example, you are visiting someone's home and when hanging your coat in the closet you immediately smell

The Human Scent Attraction

mothballs and hesitate because it reminds you of the old days. Now whose house do they remind you of? That's right, Grand Ma and Grand Pa's house. When you smelled the mothballs it took you back to a place and the feelings associated with that memory. A specific area in our brain, the limbic system, detects and activates our sense of smell. It holds memory and emotions. Everyone has had the experience of smelling something that suddenly brings back a memory of a place, a thing, or a time, and the emotions associated with those memories.

Most people enjoy pleasant scents and are attracted to people, places and things that smell good. When food smells good it makes us hungry, but if it smells bad we refuse to eat it. We purchase a particular soap, detergent or floor cleaner based on the scent that appeals to us. If a room smells good it makes you want to sit down and stay awhile. When your spiritual perfume is appealing you will notice you attract people of all colors, shapes and sizes. Jesus' spiritual perfume was so attractive that crowds in the multitudes of thousands were drawn to Him.

When Jesus came into a city He made sure to leave His fragrance behind because the aroma produced healing, deliverance, joy and peace. He left His fragrance behind so people would remember the Man from a little town call Nazareth. The town was so small people said, "Can *any* good thing come out of Nazareth?" The answer is yes. Jesus Christ the Anointed One came out of Nazareth. People may say the same thing about you. They may feel you are small or come from a small or insignificant background. Be confident in knowing your perfume was applied in small places but it can take you into large places because your gift will make room for you and will bring you before great men. David was anointed king in his father's back yard but he reigned over all of Israel.

The Human Scent Attraction

Rate Your Attractive Characteristics

Circle only one of the numbers below (0-9) for each statement; with a rating scale of **9** being the highest and best, **0** being the lowest.

I make wise decisions	0	1	2	3	4	5	6	7	8	9
I am pure	0	1	2	3	4	5	6	7	8	9
I like to smile	0	1	2	3	4	5	6	7	8	9
I am caring	0	1	2	3	4	5	6	7	8	9
I am truthful	0	1	2	3	4	5	6	7	8	9
I am joyful	0	1	2	3	4	5	6	7	8	9
I am peaceful	0	1	2	3	4	5	6	7	8	9
I am patient	0	1	2	3	4	5	6	7	8	9
I am firm in my beliefs	0	1	2	3	4	5	6	7	8	9
I am kind	0	1	2	3	4	5	6	7	8	9
I am courageous	0	1	2	3	4	5	6	7	8	9
I am focused	0	1	2	3	4	5	6	7	8	9
I am helpful to others	0	1	2	3	4	5	6	7	8	9
I am a great listener	0	1	2	3	4	5	6	7	8	9
I have positive conversations	0	1	2	3	4	5	6	7	8	9
I am a good judge of character	0	1	2	3	4	5	6	7	8	9
I regularly attend and support my church	0	1	2	3	4	5	6	7	8	9

Add up every number you circled from each statement and then add 17 to that total (17 is the total number of statements), which will give your overall score.

If your score was ***115 or above*** you are highly anointed with a beautiful fragrance.

The Human Scent Attraction

If your score was **between 85 and 114** you are slightly above average and smelling very good.

If your score was **between 70 and 84** you are just below average and you need to make some spiritual adjustments before your fragrance begins to stink.

If your score was **between 60 and 69** you are in the danger zone. You have several defects in your fragrance and you need a fresh anointing from Jesus.

If your score was **below 55** your perfume is no good. Return to Jesus and get some more oil.

Smell and the Mind

Some odors even to this day remind me of things from the past. Growing up in the South (Picayune, Mississippi) some mornings I would wake up to the mouth watering smell of bacon, eggs and coffee. On those particular mornings my parents would be in an exceptionally good mood, which caused everyone else in the house to conform to the happy atmosphere. The smell of bacon, eggs and coffee still makes me feel happy because of those memories. The sense of smell is very powerful in both the natural and spiritual realm. As a matter of fact, taste is 75% smell. A good sense of smell enhances the flavors of food and drink. Remember your last cold? When your nose was stuffy and you were unable to breathe, your food didn't have much taste.

The sense of smell plays an important role in our sense of well-being and the quality of our lives. The ability to smell brings us into oneness with nature; it warns us of possible dangers and sharpens our awareness of the people, places and things around us. It would be hard to truly appreciate a hot old-fashioned apple pie if you could not smell it first. Without the power of smell the appeal of that pie decreases by up to 75%.

The power of smell helps us respond to the people we meet. It can

The Human Scent Attraction

influence our mood, our way of thinking and what we think of others. Smell helps us determine how long to remain in any given place or even who not to sit next to. If someone on a train stinks as if he hadn't showered in weeks or smells like urine and alcohol or worse, then the likelihood of someone sitting next to him is very slim because the ability to smell tells their brain **do not sit there**. If you go into a house that smells like gas from the stove you would not go inside and strike a match because your sense of smell tells your mind there is danger.

So many sisters have said to me "Pastor why do men run from me as if I was a burning building?" The first thing I say is, "Be glad they run now instead of making a commitment then leave later". The second is, "They may sense or smell something that is out of place with you". Maybe they felt you could not be trusted, or you may be too far ahead of him. Remember I said in the first chapter that all smells are attractive. Smell lures things to a place and people to people. Could your scent be the reason why no good men are coming to you? Something about the way you smell spiritually attracts certain men to you or, never brings them to you at all.

Do you see how important smell is, how it causes us respond? It is essential for you to have on the glorious fragrance of the Lord and not one that smells like danger. The man of God, who walks after the Holy Spirit, will respond to your spiritual fragrance.

Chapter 8

The Bible's Beauty Secret

For the LORD delights in his people; he beautifies the humble with salvation.

> *Psalm 149:4 (New Living Translation)*

*L*et's face it; we all could use a little help in the good looks department.

If that statement were not true all cosmetic stores would go out of business and so would cosmetic surgeons. Every time I see a celebrity on the cover of a magazine or on TV without make up it surprises me how different they look. You would be amazed how much time and money people spend on looking good. Attractive people know looking good has its benefits and so does the Lord. That is why the Lord promised to put beauty in you and on you with His salvation (Psalm 149:4).

The beauty of salvation covers the woman who humbles herself before God, realizing she owes everything to Him and all she will become must pass through Him. That spirit of reliance and dependency on God causes Him to lift you up into the high places. One of the Old Testament names of God is **El Elyon,** the Most High God. When a small child hugs your legs then looks at you with his arms held upward, you immediately know what he wants from you. That's right, he wants to be picked up and lifted to a higher place, a safe place, close to your face. Seeing we serve the Most High God there is no reason for us to live Most Low. God desires to give us the high places that are manifold demonstrations of His blessings. These high places are so full of favor and grace that:

> *Give, and it shall be given unto you; good measure, pressed down, and shaken together, and running over, shall men give*

The Bible's Beauty Secret

into your bosom.

Luke 6:38 (KJV)

Most women wear high heel shoes to give them a lift, helping them to be noticed better; plus the shoes look good with their outfit. In the same way humble women are blessed with spiritual fragrances, gifts and fruit of the Spirit in order to exalt them above the proud and make them more noticeable and easier to find. Jesus said if you pray in your closet your answers will come to you before all but when you pray before all to be seen; you already have your reward. The closet is not a glamorous place. It is humbling, so that way He answers you in a glamorous manner before other people.

Humility is not walking around with your head down, never accepting compliments, never saying anything good about yourself or letting people walk all over you treating you any kind of way. That is false humility. Real men feel good about a woman with self-assurance who is not in constant need of encouragement and validation. True humility is dependence on God. When humility is acted upon it produces strength. A real life example was Jesus who humbled himself before God while facing a violent death, yet He never opened His mouth against His persecutors. That is strength. That is humility. God has, therefore, highly exalted Jesus, giving Him a name above very name, that at the name of Jesus every knee shall bow and every tongue confess that Jesus is Lord to the glory and honor of God the Father (Philippians 2:9-11).

If you truly desire to be beautiful and have a fragrance that will assist the man of God in finding you, then stay in a posture of prayer and live in the spirit of humility. God promises to make you attractive with salvation (deliverance, overcoming power and the desires of your heart).

Hard Ain't Pretty

When a man is searching for a wife he is not looking for another man. Men are not looking for replicas of themselves. Men want feminine, soft, pleasant and graceful wives just like women are looking for a real man. What woman desires to have a soft prissy man who is afraid of getting his

The Bible's Beauty Secret

nails dirty, racing to the nail salon for a manicure, or a man who goes to the beauty supply store for himself and not you, or pays to get his hair done and not yours? A manly man will sacrifice his own needs to make sure his beautiful wife has her needs met. Every single man out there is looking for a woman with the right spirit. If you have the right spirit whatever he has is yours with no hesitation. It is in our nature as men to sacrifice and give to the woman who has our heart.

[21] Submitting yourselves one to another in the fear of God.

[22] Wives, submit yourselves unto your own husbands, as unto the Lord.

[23] For the husband is the head of the wife, even as Christ is the Head of the church: and he is the Savior of the body.

[24] Therefore as the church is subject unto Christ, so let the wives be to their own husbands in every thing.

[25] Husbands, <u>love your wives</u>, even <u>as Christ</u> also loved the church, and <u>gave himself for it</u>;

Ephesians 5:21-25 (KJV)

No, the Bible is not telling you to be a doormat to your husband. You are his comforter-helper standing firmly by his side and not under his feet. As you can see in verse 25 he will love you and give of himself for you, if you have the right spirit – a submissive spirit.

If you are trying to be stronger than him and trying to be the head of the relationship, not only are you playing out of position, but also more importantly you are losing the game. Being out of character by commanding him, running things and never submitting to his God-given

The Bible's Beauty Secret

position is too demanding for any man, regardless of his race, nationality, background or upbringing.

Don't be selfish. If he is giving himself, time and money then the least you can do is see what he desires. What does he need? What does he desire in his heart? Find out and then seek to fulfill it. Does he want dinner at a specific time? Does he want you in bed with him at a certain time? If your husband is sacrificing for you, it is your job to see about him and his needs with a meek spirit.

It is becoming a real task to tell the difference between boys and girls and men and women in this generation. Girls want to be hard and rough and the boys want to be soft and dainty. What kind of spirit are we dealing with? Even in the church some of the women speakers take the podium and lose touch with their femininity transforming into a she-man. The male preachers are flipping their hands around and rolling their eyes and necks; it's hard to get a good firm handshake from some of these softies. What type of message are we sending?

A humble spirit is like a mountain made of gold, priceless and rare. You also will be this valuable, once you walk in a spirit of meekness.

[1] Likewise, ye wives,
be in subjection to your own husbands;
that if any obey not the word,
they also may without the word
be won by the conversation of the wives;

[2] While they behold your chaste conversation
coupled with fear.

[3] Whose adorning let it not be that
outward adorning of plaiting the hair,
and of wearing of gold,
or of putting on of apparel:

[4] But let it be the hidden man of the heart,

The Bible's Beauty Secret

in that which is not corruptible,
*even the ornament of a **meek** and **quiet spirit**,*
which is in the sight of God of great price.

I Peter 3:1-4 (KJV)

The Proud Woman's Plague

When you know you look good that can lead to an attitude of vanity. Some women are too attractive for their own good. They trust in their good looks to make things happen for them. In most cases when they think they have it altogether the spirit of pride begins to move; even upon the bold and the beautiful, especially if they have not humbled themselves before the Lord. Pride is a very deceptive spirit that can prevent your life from progressing forward. Unless you examine yourself for evidence of conceit it can go unnoticed for many years, hindering your life.

What areas of your life have not been given to God? What decisions do you make without seeking God first, like selecting male friends, dating, accepting gifts or letting your friends pick someone for you? Even those decisions are full of pride because you have not allowed Jesus to be Lord over your relationships. Pride is thinking you can do everything or even certain things without God. The spirit of pride even refuses to acknowledge the existence to God. This is exactly why God sees proud people as His enemy instead of His children.

> *God resists the proud but He gives grace or **favor** to the humble.*
>
> *James 4:6 (New Living Translation)*

> *The Lord will tear down the house of the proud but he will protect the belongings of the widow.*
>
> *Proverbs 15:25 (New Living Translation)*

Have you ever wondered why so many good-looking women, no matter how attractive, are plagued by bad relationships or have no relationship at all? You would think they could attract the best men, but to the contrary,

The Bible's Beauty Secret

they draw the worst kinds because of the spirit of pride.

Women who do not value themselves enough to demand honesty, faithfulness and respect in a relationship are spoiling men. Even worse, these women allow them to have others on the side and sometimes share their bed just to please the man. How degrading. What a serious threat to the Spiritual Woman because these men expect they can treat you the same way and you should just be happy he comes home to you every other night. Most men who refuse to follow the ways of the Lord view relationships with women as a game (he's a player), not taken seriously; there are plenty of these men in the church also. The more attractive you are the better the game; so instead of a two-point shot, getting an attractive woman is more like a three-pointer. Pretty women with pride have a tendency to hook up with men who are no good at all and everyone can see it but them. The cycle will continue until she humbles herself before the Lord.

Chapter 9

Good Women with Bad Men

Good women have great things going for them but for some reason many end up with the short end of the stick in relationships. It is not surprising to find most of these good women are very faithful, loyal, strong in spirit and mightily used of the Lord. They encourage others and pray their sisters through but they themselves seem to attract men who appear to be good at first, yet turn out to be just like the last man they were involved with.

Some women start out well but end badly because they have been played and then become players themselves. Some women are sneaking around with married men and even celebrate that he treats her better than his wife. In some warped way they feel special when married men prefer them, being so desperate they cannot think clearly.

Let me tell you this: the road to Good Marriage Destiny is actually a series of decisions. If you sleep with him you could lose him and if you don't sleep with him you might lose him. What will you do? If you decide to sleep with someone else's husband you have chosen to release a curse on your own destiny; when and if you get married, your man will be the type to cheat on you. Be careful, even if the curse does not fall on you, your daughters are watching and learn by your example.

If married buzzards are circling around then there is something about you that is dead, which is nothing to be proud of because it exposes a serious spiritual defect. When married men start coming to you it is not the time to exchange phone numbers but to self-evaluate and take a spiritual inventory to see what is alive and what is dead. The unclean spirit inside tells you *"If she (his wife) was handling her business he wouldn't come to me"*, thus

Good Women with Bad Men

causing you to think what you have to offer him is better; but of course, that is a lie. Married people who cheat on their spouses fall into the plan of Satan to form a scene for a crime of passion by having a love triangle. In most love triangles one or two will end up dying and in some cases all have died, in the natural and the spiritual.

For some women it seems as though every Mr. Right turns out to be a devil in disguise. What is it? Is it you? Is it them? Is it the town you live in or the church you attend? The answer to all of these could very well be an emphatic YES. Not all relationships turn sour because of the man, sometimes the problem is the woman, and perhaps she is not good at selecting men. Maybe the men in your town are spoiled by all the attention from women and just aren't willing to commit to one person. Maybe where you live is being depleted of men because of crime and imprisonment, death, or quite possibly a rise in homosexuality. Maybe it's the church you attend. You could have a wonderful Pastor but no one is getting married and single men do not attend. Outwardly these seem to be logical solutions but not all cases are so conclusive. Maybe it is none of the above. The most common case for this issue is the woman's spiritual odor. Could it be your spiritual scent is drawing these hungry hounds and stray dogs to your front porch? Can they smell a defect in your spiritual aroma? Do they sense something in the spirit realm that you are not even aware of?

It is possible to overcome this dilemma; here is an example. A woman in my congregation persevered and kept her spiritual scent strong and pure. She met a minister from Seattle while attending a women's retreat and they continued to talk long distance about the word of God. She kept telling him about the word being preached at my church. Finally, he had to hear for himself and flew into town. One Sunday morning she walked into my office with a big smile on her face saying 'Pastor there's someone I want you to meet'. We talked for a few minutes and then I went out into the pulpit and I spoke the word God gave me for that day, I think it was entitled "Pregnant by the Wrong Man". The brother was so blessed and excited he told me if she has been under this kind of teaching she is going to be a wonderful wife. The next week they were engaged.

Good Women with Bad Men

I Hear You Crying

I have conducted meetings, conferences and revivals where sisters come well dressed but depressed, looking good but feeling bad, smiling outwardly but sobbing in sorrow inwardly, appearing whole and happy but are broken inside thinking to themselves "If God doesn't do something for me tonight I just might break and go Coo-Coo for Coco puffs". Some of them are anointed enough to pray for and heal the pains of others but are dying inside from a broken and lonely heart. This is one of the classic works of Satan against single women in the church.

Often before ministering I look over the crowd and listen to the room. Sometimes I can hear women crying out to God in their spirits for deliverance from bad relationships. They have no one to relate with, no one to love, and no one who can reassure them of their beauty and their value. They come to the church hoping God will give a Prophetic Word concerning their relational dilemma; hoping for a Word of Wisdom to lead them step-by-step, take them by the hand in the Spirit and walk them out. Some are hoping to hear a clear, healing and anointed Word from God until the presence of the Lord fills the house with breakthrough power; thus freeing them from evil soul-ties.

When I hear the cry of the hurting, lonely and confused women in the church I am assured at that very moment the Lord has certainly heard it far before I did and He is doing something about it **now**. These women have questions like "How do I get over him? How am I going to make it without him? Who will want me? How do I break my connection (soul-tie) to him? Will I ever get married? When is he coming? Where is he coming from? Why hasn't God sent my husband yet? Where are the good men? Why are all the men in my life so weak, sorry and childish?" or simply, "Jesus what's up??!!'"

This is why the men and women of God must be wise, discerning, confrontational and equipped with more power and resources than people of the world. We cannot preach a one-dimensional word because people have complex issues, problems and feelings. People are under the influence of the demonic and need a move of the Lord's Spirit to set them

Good Women with Bad Men

free. Some issues are generational (passed down through the blood line) some are seasonal (coming upon people at set times), some are self induced (brought on by the actions of the individual), but their problems will not disappear while we preach a pretty word to people with ugly problems. We must preach the Gospel with demonstrations of the Power of Jesus. Many in this present day need to experience deliverance God's way.

Many times it is the message we **don't** preach that harms the hurting ones. I have personally been a member of churches where the leaders never prayed for single people nor preached or taught on the single Christian life, when most churches have an abundance of single women. If you are single I command you in the Name of Jesus to be empowered, encouraged and anointed with the fragrance of the Lord right now. I speak healing to your mind and rebuke every negative voice from invading your spirit. Open your ears so you can hear the voice of Jesus the Good Shepherd.

Test Rate Your Spiritual Scent (Part 1)

1. Have you accepted Jesus Christ into your heart and received Him as Lord and Savior?

2. Have you been baptized with the Holy Ghost since you believed?

3. Do you speak in other tongues?

4. Do you handle the truth well?

5. Do you have a consistent Bible reading program?

6. Do you attend church and other worship services more than once a week?

7. Do you communicate well with others?

8. Are you submissive to spiritual authority?

9. Do you regularly attend singles ministry meetings and events?

10. Do you volunteer for any of the ministries at your church?

Good Women with Bad Men

11. Do you pray at least three hours a week?

12. Do you truly respect what the Bible says about your body being the temple of the Holy Ghost?

13. Do you have a pleasant personality?

14. Do you have hobbies? (If yes, please list 3)

15. Do you help others in need?

16. Do you pray for others?

17. Are you a soul winner for the Lord?

18. Do you love yourself?

If you answered **no to only one of the questions** your spiritual scent is very strong, your husband will discover you soon.

If you answered **no to two or three** of the questions your fragrance is lacking some oil. You are in need of a fresh anointing of the Spirit of the Lord.

If you answered **no to four or more** of the questions you have very little spiritual fragrance and are lacking in the areas of commitment and concern. You need more of Christ in your life before you can be ready for a growing and meaningful relationship.

Test Rate Your Spiritual Scent (Part 2)

1. Do you date often?

2. If your friends or those closest to you were asked if you were a flirt, would they say yes or no?

3. Do you think tight fitting or revealing clothes bring out the best in you?

4. Are you a moody person?

5. Do you dislike or mistreat yourself?

Good Women with Bad Men

6.   Do you carry any bitterness from past relationships?

7.   Are you still hurting from an old relationship?

8.   Are you angry at the opposite sex for any reason?

9.   Do you think you are desperate?

If you answered **no to all** of the questions from Part 2 your scent for this chapter is excellent.

If you answered **yes to two** of these your scent is good but can improve.

If you answered **yes to four or more** your spiritual scent is bad and you are in need of a new anointing.

PRAYER

Father in the name of Jesus I give you glory for your wisdom, provision and protection.

I am shielded and covered from those who wish to harm me. A thousand shall fall at my left hand and on my right but they will not come nigh me.

Father I humble myself under your mighty hand, saying not my will but thy will be done.

Lord I thank you for a beautiful spirit, heart and mind. You have beautified me with your salvation, deliverance and glory.

I trust you will send a soul mate into my life that has your heart inside him like a wheel in the middle of a wheel.

I'm blessed because you said I'm blessed.
In Jesus' name. Amen

Chapter 10

Your Spiritual Virginity

12 A garden inclosed is my sister, my spouse; a spring shut up, a fountain sealed. 13 Thy plants are an orchard of pomegranates...

Song of Solomon 4:12-13 (KJV)

Therefore if any man be in Christ he is a new creature.

II Corinthians 5:17 (KJV)

Virgin (Heb. *bethulah*, lit. "separated"; Gk. *parthenos*), in the Old Testament a woman who has not had sexual intercourse with a man.

Young Mary the mother of Jesus was engaged to a man named Joseph and she was noted in scripture as being a virgin. God chose Mary because of her purity, being from the bloodline of David (Luke 1:27) and faith (Matthew 1:18-23). God is very selective about where He places His heavenly gifts. He does not give His blessing to any and every place nor to any and everybody. If God is going to send something from heaven then that person, place or thing must first be sanctified. God sends preachers, prophets, and evangelists to sanctify you with the washing of the water of the Word; and then you will see the promises of the Word manifest (Ephesians 5:26-27).

Read the following verse about the manna from heaven in the wilderness and see if you can identify God's pattern of blessing.

*13 And it came to pass, that at even the quails came up, and covered the camp: and in the morning the **dew lay***

116

Your Spiritual Virginity

*round about the host. [14] And when the **dew that lay was
gone up**, behold, upon the face of the wilderness there **lay
a small round thing**, as small as the hoar frost on the
ground. [15] And when the children of Israel saw it, they said
one to another, It is manna: for they wist not what it was.*

Exodus 16:13-15 (KJV)

As you can see from the verse above God would not send Bread from
heaven until the ground was first washed and cleansed by the dew from
heaven. Once the dew was taken up, God was willing to send Bread to
meet the needs of the masses in the wilderness.

I believe Jesus' birth in a manger was the work of God. He was put in the
feeding trough for animals because there was no room for Him at the inn
(Luke 2:7). It was there in the manger that God trusted the actions of
animals more than that of the people at the inn.

Do you want the blessings of the Lord to fall on you? Do you want God to
send what you need and the thing you have been asking Him for? Follow
His pattern.

God will not send anything from heaven unless there is a place set aside to
lay it down. Elisabeth had to conceive her baby, John the Baptist, before
Mary could become pregnant by the Holy Ghost (Luke 1:13-37). Before
Jesus could complete His mission on earth, His cousin John the Baptist
had to be His forerunner (Malachi 3:1). If you are looking for God to send
you a blessing from heaven then you must sanctify yourself, because He
will not send you heaven's best for the earth's worst. The blessing must
land on sanctified ground.

The king celebrates the virginity of his new bride in Song of Solomon
4:12 by saying his wife was a garden enclosed, a spring shut up and a
fountain sealed. The word orchard in Hebrew means *pardes*; "a forest,
park or paradise". It also flows with the Greek word *paradeisos*; meaning
"park, Eden or paradise". Whether male or female, your virginity is a
precious gift to the husband or wife that is so highly privileged to receive

it. King Solomon said his wife's virginity was a paradise like the Garden of Eden. My sister, your virginity is a treasure to which only your husband should have the key. It is somewhere only he can go to be refreshed and blessed by the fruit of his private garden.

Archeologists have searched endlessly for the Garden of Eden but failed miserably in their attempts. They have spent millions of dollars for centuries trying to find it. That should speak to every woman of God. Your private garden is so valuable that men will search the jungles and wilderness to find you. It should also tell you finding a woman who is keeping her garden free of unlawful intruders is a rare occurrence. Private Gardens are hard to find; whether inside the church or out, because many have gone wild. Some gardens have been invaded, inhabited, visited, vacated and uncovered, even touched and turned repeatedly like a doorknob. These high traffic gardens represent women who are sexually active. They decrease in value because they are easily accessed and everybody knows about them. That is not attractive to a potential husband.

A Second Chance

Lately there has been a lot of talk in worldly circles about secondary virginity. Secondary virginity is a personal decision to refrain from further sexual activity until marriage. It is seen as an opportunity to leave the past behind and start over, which is exactly what the Bible teaches. However, I will show you the difference between the world's teaching on secondary virginity and the Bible's view on spiritual virginity.

The world teaches secondary virginity is a time to change bad habits and heal past wounds, allowing for self-renewal before marriage. I think this is the world's way of coming close to spiritual virginity. The world's teaching, although it offers a second chance, leaves the cleansing and changing to the individual. The Bible's spiritual virginity gives the individual a second chance and reveals the power of the new creature through Christ according to II Corinthians 5:17.

The value of a second chance is amazing, more important than the initial

Your Spiritual Virginity

start or the very beginning. In your initial start you may think you have forever and time will never run out so you waste it. You don't realize how important it is until it's all gone.

Have you ever used a pencil without an eraser? If you made a mistake you would have to mark it and wait until you found an eraser or try to trace over what you've written, making matters worse. That small piece of rubber on top of the pencil gives the writer an opportunity to make changes after mistakes. The inventor must have taken this to heart knowing people make mistakes and need a way to remove them. God has an eraser and it's called the **Blood of Jesus**, which washes us whiter than snow.

People do not realize the importance and value of what they have until it is taken away, leaving behind a feeling of regret, wishing they could start all over again. Thank God we don't have to wish because God has made it possible to start over. All of us have a past filled with sins, mistakes, disobedience and bad decisions. It is important to know we cannot live in the past because Jesus saved us from our past. We must live in the present with faithful expectation toward our future. You may say 'I'm not a virgin and will never regain that again'. That may be true in the natural but not in the spiritual. Your flesh will never be a virgin again but in the spirit realm you are made a new creature being born again.

> *Therefore if anyone is in Christ, he is a new creature; the old things passed away; behold, new things have come.*

> *II Corinthians 5:17 (New Living Translation)*

Second chances are not always recognizable because they can sometimes take us to the back of the line when we would rather start from the place where we fell. We don't realize we've been given a second chance, especially when we have suffered a loss. After some time, thought, prayer and grace you come to realize 'this is a second chance for me'. Adam and Eve received a second chance when they were kicked out of the Garden and forced to live in a land of thorns and thistles. To most people that seemed a harsh punishment from God but to the Christian we

Your Spiritual Virginity

see a second chance. True punishment would have been an immediate death sentence, but this gave them a new start from a new place. It was God's grace that removed them from the garden, preventing further damage.

> *21 Unto Adam also and to his wife did the LORD God make coats of skins, and clothed them. 22 And the LORD God said, Behold, the man is become as one of us, to know good and evil: and now, lest he put forth his hand, and take also of the tree of life, and eat, and live for ever: 23 Therefore the LORD God sent him forth from the garden of Eden, to till the ground from whence he was taken. 24 So he drove out the man; and he placed at the east of the garden of Eden Cherubims, and a flaming sword which turned every way, to keep the way of the tree of life.*

> *Genesis 3:21-24 (KJV)*

Adam and Eve's removal from the garden was grace at its best. Yes they were sent to an undesirable place, but it was still a second chance for the fallen couple. Their removal was not done in divine anger, but divine grace. Notice before God removed them from the place of their mistake He showed His willingness to clean up their mess by making coats of animal skins. Instead of pouring on the guilt and condemnation God met their need.

Seeing you have been granted a second chance, sanctify your body as unto the Lord. God has sanctified you by laying aside your old self with her past deeds; He has instead risen up a new person with a new heart and mind.

Most men who are attracted to your spiritual fragrance are willing to accept the fact you had a past before coming to the Lord. They may not be so willing if they discover your behavior and attitudes have not changed even after giving your life to the Lord. Once you give your life to Jesus, keep the new you pure and undefiled. Now your spiritual virginity can be given as a sweet smelling gift to your future husband. You must

Your Spiritual Virginity

not defile the new you that is made in the image of Christ, and not after the fallen nature of Adam. In Adam there is failure and a tendency to disobey. In Christ Jesus you are more than a conqueror, desiring to obey with all of your heart, soul and mind.

In the parable of the ten virgins, the five foolish ones had the same opportunity as the wise but were careless with their time and made no preparations to meet the bridegroom (Matthew 25:1-13). Even today there remain wise and foolish among us. Some choose to make the most of what has been given them and others will just waste it all away as if they had plenty of time and many more opportunities, not realizing both time and opportunity ultimately run out. Guard your spiritual virginity (the new man / new creature) with wisdom and great diligence. Remember, this is your second chance.

Chapter 11

Fragrance Haters

*I*f the men around you can't wait until marriage then they ain't nothing but fragrance haters. Congratulate yourself on keeping it together while maintaining and strengthening your fragrance, fruit and gifts.

If all they want to do is to sample your fragrance while not appreciating your chastity, dedication and dreams of holy matrimony, then they are nothing more than haters. They desire to take your lovely spiritual fragrance and put some funk in it. Funk is defilement through sexual activity outside of marriage. Once they have defiled the fragrance it is good for nothing but to be put under the feet of men (Matthew 5:13). It might feel good in the natural but it doesn't smell good in the spirit. In contrast, when you have sex with your husband your fragrance is not defiled, instead it remains clean and holy.

> *Marriage is honourable in all, and the bed undefiled: but whoremongers and adulterers God will judge.*
>
> *Hebrews 13:4 (KJV)*

You may have times when you desire to be intimate with someone, but you must choose to be steadfast and unmovable until the Lord draws your husband to you. It is far too expensive to waste on a fragrance hater, a sampler, a prodigal (wasteful) son, a fly-by-night or dead man. A man who is only after sex does not care about your spiritual fragrance nor does he care about the price that was paid for your cleansing. He does not take into consideration that you have been keeping yourself for marriage. He is only concerned with sampling your perfume just to say he knows what it smells like and then leave you to deal with the messy results.

Fragrance Haters

The fragrance hater may offer to pay some of your bills, take you shopping or to a nice restaurant. They may even go to church with you for a while, but be careful. Be alert; be vigilant for your adversary the devil is seeking to devour and destroy. Beware of fragrance haters who come to you in the name of love but always produce pain and hatred in the end. They come in the name of friendship but leave you broken and alone. They are wolves in sheep's clothing. Paul said, "I am writing you in tears as I get ready to depart this world because I know when I leave greedy wolves will come in among you" (Acts 20:29). Fan them away from you or they will become a fly in your ointment. I will go into further detail about flies later on.

Other women may not understand why you are acting differently; not having their same attitude towards men or even regarding men another way in your conversation. They may become jealous of your new commitment. Regardless of what other women do, even your closest friends, stay true to the call of God for your life. It may seem they are having fun and enjoying life with men, but they are actually being spoiled, stained, tainted and ruined by the very men who claim to love them. Once the men they are sleeping with are finished with them it will take years to recover from the devastation and spiritual damage. Not many men are running to the altar with women who have reputations for going to bed with several men. Take it from a man's perspective; keep your oil pure and clean for your future husband.

Tamar and Her Fragrance Haters

Have you noticed how people everywhere make fun of and even dislike virgins or committed people? Virgins and the committed are being laughed at and called L-7's, corny, weird and stupid. The world hates people who aren't having sex outside of marriage and tries with all its might to get those people to break their commitment. The world's system does not understand nor does it appreciate the system of the Kingdom of God. As follower's of Christ, it is our desire that His Kingdom come and that His will be done on earth as it is in heaven (Matthew 6:10).

Television, comedy shows, movies, schoolteachers and even pastors and leaders in the church make fun of virgins. You would think church is where chastity would be preached, taught, exemplified, and celebrated; not fragrance hated. Nevertheless don't give in the to the mind games coming your way. The world, the devil and the flesh will test you, pressuring you into an unholy decision that may abort God's plan and purpose for your life. Submit yourself to God's will for your life; resist the devil and he will flee from you (James 4:7). You will have the last laugh if you stand your ground. You will be blessed if you stand. You will be strengthened if you stand. You will be satisfied with a husband from the Lord if you stand. Stand in the pain, stand in the midst of loneliness, stand in the heartache, stand even in the shame. Let the tears flow, but stand. Weeping may endure for a night but JOY (satisfaction) is coming in the morning. Joy is coming. Joy is coming. Joy is coming in a moment.

Many oysters are waiting to be devoured on someone's dinner plate, but a pearl will stand the test of time. Do you know what an oyster goes through before it becomes a beautiful, high priced and valuable pearl? A small grain of sand gets into the oyster's shell while feeding. That small grain of sand is like a sharp razor to the oyster's tender flesh. Once the sand is inside it begins cutting the oyster with its sharp jagged edges. The oyster's flesh then coats that grain continually until the end result is a precious pearl. It endures intense pain as it transforms from being just an ordinary oyster to something of greater value. What seems to us like a mistake, a case of misfortune and a bad circumstance is working for the oyster's good. How could this have happened to an innocent little oyster? I'll tell you, it happened by divine design in order to make something greater.

Let me tell you this, when God has plans to take something or someone to the next level, He lets a grain of sand in **on purpose** to advance you from the ordinary places in life to the high places of His holy purpose. Joseph could only dream of being great until God let the sand in on him (Genesis 37:5-9). Joseph's brothers got rid of him and made his disappearance look as though an animal had eaten him. Joseph told them they meant it for evil but God meant if for good (Genesis 50:20). He went to jail for something he did not do. He went through hell for years but hell couldn't hold him, it only cut until the appointed time. He became a pearl and never felt the

Fragrance Haters

pain of sand again.

God is allowing your current situation for your own good. Your lonely days may be a grain of sand, your brokenness may be a grain of sand; it is not meant to kill you but instead make you greater. Inside the oyster that grain of sand cuts with every movement. The oyster, reacting in pain moves again and the sand cuts it over and over again. It secretes a white colored fluid that aids in healing but because the sand remains inside and continues to cut; the secretion continues until there is no oyster left, only the secretion that hardens and is now called a pearl. The oyster had to endure intense physical pain but now look at it; it doesn't look the same or feel the same and its value has greatly increased.

I gave this illustration to show if you endure the pain as the sand cuts you will come out of the ordeal worth so much more. You will become the pearl of the Lord and a valuable jewel to your husband. This is the time of your transformation. You are being taken through the process of God. You cannot afford to give in to the pressure because it is the desire of the devil to ruin your future. The devil is a hater and will send fragrance haters to ruin your holy destiny.

King David's daughter Tamar was loved and hated by her brother Amnon (a fragrance hater).

> [1] *And it came to pass after this, that Absalom the son of David had a fair sister, whose name was Tamar; and Amnon the son of David loved her.* [2] *And Amnon was so vexed, that he fell sick for his sister Tamar; for she was a virgin; and Amnon thought it hard for him to do any thing to her.* [3] *But Amnon had a friend, whose name was Jonadab, the son of Shimeah David's brother: and Jonadab was a very subtil man.* [4] *And he said unto him, Why art thou, being the king's son, lean from day to day? wilt thou not tell me? And Amnon said unto him, I love Tamar, my brother Absalom's sister.* [5] *And Jonadab said unto him, Lay thee down on thy bed, and make thyself sick: and when thy father cometh to see thee, say unto him, I*

Fragrance Haters

pray thee, let my sister Tamar come, and give me meat, and dress the meat in my sight, that I may see it, and eat it at her hand. [6] So Amnon lay down, and made himself sick: and when the king was come to see him, Amnon said unto the king, I pray thee, let Tamar my sister come, and make me a couple of cakes in my sight, that I may eat at her hand. [7] Then David sent home to Tamar, saying, Go now to thy brother Amnon's house, and dress him meat. [8] So Tamar went to her brother Amnon's house; and he was laid down. And she took flour , and kneaded it, and made cakes in his sight, and did bake the cakes. [9] And she took a pan, and poured them out before him; but he refused to eat. And Amnon said, Have out all men from me. And they went out every man from him. [10] And Amnon said unto Tamar, Bring the meat into the chamber, that I may eat of thine hand. And Tamar took the cakes which she had made, and brought them into the chamber to Amnon her brother. [11] And when she had brought them unto him to eat, he took hold of her, and said unto her, Come lie with me, my sister. [12] And she answered him, Nay, my brother, do not force me; for no such thing ought to be done in Israel: do not thou this folly. [13] And I, whither shall I cause my shame to go? and as for thee, thou shalt be as one of the fools in Israel. Now therefore, I pray, speak unto the king; for he will not withhold me from thee. [14] Howbeit he would not hearken unto her voice: but, being stronger than she, forced her, and lay with her. [15] Then **_Amnon hated her exceedingly_** *;* **_so that the hatred wherewith he hated her was greater than the love wherewith he had loved her._** *And Amnon said unto her, Arise, be gone. [16] And she said unto him, There is no cause: this evil in sending me away is greater than the other that thou didst unto me. But he would not hearken unto her. [17] Then he called his servant that ministered unto him, and said, Put now this woman out from me, and bolt the door after her. [18] And she had a garment of divers colours upon her: for with such robes were the king's*

Fragrance Haters

daughters that were virgins apparelled. Then his servant brought her out, and bolted the door after her. [19] And Tamar put ashes on her head, and rent her garment of divers colours that was on her, and laid her hand on her head, and went on crying. [20] And Absalom her brother said unto her, Hath Amnon thy brother been with thee?

2 Samuel 13:1-20 (KJV)

David had a beautiful virgin daughter by the name of Tamar; she is the first Tamar I will highlight. Tamar and her parents were very careful about protecting the honor of her virginity; whenever she left the house she had a host of handmaidens (virgin servants) with her. I think that is a good idea for you. I know you are an adult, but you should have at least two or three witnesses of your good behavior, plus you can hold each other accountable. Tamar wore a beautiful dress of many colors given by her father, which proudly announced to the public that she was a virgin daughter of the king. The many colors spoke of the spiritual fragrance of virginity, spiritual fruit and gifts of the Spirit upon her because of her dedication. Seeing her dress brought uncommitted women to an open shame. That is a portrait of you; you are the daughter of the **King of Kings** and you have been vested with a spiritual garment that says you are the virgin of the **LORD of Lords**.

And she had a garment of divers colours upon her: for with such robes were the king's daughters that were virgins apparelled.
2 Samuel 13:18 (KJV)

Tamar was the sister of Absalom. The Bible lets us know Absalom cared greatly for his sister Tamar because they had the same mother who was a princess of Geshur by the name of Maach, one of David's wives (2 Samuel 3:3).

Tamar was set up by her half brother Amnon who was so obsessed that he literally became sick with desire for her. The Bible says he loved her but it is only stating the difference between true love and lust. Once Amnon

Fragrance Haters

took what he wanted, he did a complete turnaround and the Bible says he hated her more than he ever loved her. There is a difference between the two. Amnon was a true fragrance hater. He wanted to rob Tamar of her fragrance so badly he would not eat; suffering from a physical and psychological love spell, but it was all based on hatred. Many women have discovered this same type of spirit in men who wanted them so badly they even cried, begged, bought expensive gifts, played with the kids and made all kinds of promises in order to get them. After having sex the phone calls stopped and the attitude changed; it was like an about face, a complete 180-degree turn.

Love is patient, love is kind, love does not behave itself unseemly, it seeketh not its own (not selfish) I Corinthians 13. God is the greatest example of Love "For God **so** *(*the measure of His love*)* loved the world that He **gave**" (John 3:16). Lust on the other hand seeks to fulfill its own desire; it takes and is selfish. Lust is a sinful longing. It is inward sin that will lead to a falling away from God.

> *Then when lust hath conceived, it bringeth forth sin: and sin, when it is finished, bringeth forth death.*
>
> *James 1:15 (KJV)*

After Amnon forced himself on her the Bible says he:

> *Hated her exceedingly; so that the hatred wherewith he hated her was greater than the love wherewith he had loved her. And Amnon said unto her, Arise, be gone.*
>
> *II Samuel 13:15 (KJV)*

Needless to say, this beautiful girl with great hopes and expectations for her future had it all snatched away, by a fragrance hater. The same is taking place with many of our daughters and sisters in the Lord. Their futures are shattered and the beauty of marriage is being taken away. Tamar went into Amnon's house a virgin with glory on her life but she left with ashes on her head and a torn dress. The ashes symbolized what is left

128

after a fire, a biblical sign of destruction, mourning, and insignificance. She was never the same after her fragrance was stolen and spent the rest of her days living in shame and disgrace. "So Tamar remained desolate in her brother Absalom's house" (II Samuel 13:20). The Bible never mentions anything about her meeting a man and getting married. Her life was shut down by a hater.

Advice for Christian Dating

- Always date committed Christian men.

- Keep in mind you are trying to get to know him through conversation only. (Don't become physical).

- Ask questions about his past, present and plans for the future.

- Dress appropriately; nothing revealing that will attract sexual attention.

- Do not date frequently unless he has proposed and you have set a date.

- See each other at church functions and other public outings. Keep private intimate meetings to a minimum.

- Bring him around your spiritual leaders.

- Be honest about the flaws you notice in him (for example: cursing when upset). Never think you can fix them later, after you are married, because you can't.

- If he is not a good match do not feel obligated to date him again.

How Does God Deal with Fragrance Haters?

God has a way of dealing with fragrance haters because He realizes some men tend to develop a dislike for the woman after the deed is done. God takes the time to deal with the domestic affairs of men. It has been said police officers are slow to respond to a domestic call because they are more likely to be killed during domestic disputes. God still delights in directing the issues of men (Psalm 8:4-5).

Fragrance Haters

If any man take a wife, and **go in unto her, and** <u>**hate**</u> **her.**
*And give occasions of speech against her, and bring up
and evil name upon her, and say, I took this woman, and
when I came to her, I found her not a maid: Then shall the
father of the damsel, and her mother, take and bring forth
the tokens of the damsel's virginity unto the elders of the
city in the gate: And the damsel's father shall say unto the
elders, I gave my daughter unto this man to wife, and he
<u>**hateth**</u> her; And, lo, he hath given occasions of speech
against her, saying, I found not thy daughter a maid; and
yet these are the tokens of my daughter's virginity. And
they shall spread the cloth before the elders of the city.
And the elders of that city shall take that man and chastise
him; And they shall amerce him in an hundred shekels of
silver, and give them unto the father of the damsel, because
he hath brought up an evil name upon a virgin of Israel:
and she shall be his wife; he may not put her away all his
days.*

Deuteronomy 22:13-19 (KJV)

Tamar the Hated

The book of Genesis tells the story of the second Tamar. She was married
to two of Judah's sons. Her first husband was Er, Judah's first born. Judah
found Tamar for him but the Bible says Er was wicked in the sight of God
and the Lord killed him. What happened? What could he have done?
Could he have been a fragrance hater towards Tamar not willing to fulfill
the plan of God to be fruitful and multiply? He and Tamar never had
children. The law of the land at that time was if a man died without having
children his brother was to marry the widow and produce a child who
would bear the name of his deceased brother.

*⁶ And Judah took a wife for Er his firstborn, whose name
was Tamar. ⁷ And Er, Judah's firstborn, was wicked in the
sight of the LORD; and the LORD slew him. ⁸ And Judah
said unto Onan, Go in unto thy brother's wife, and marry
her, and raise up seed to thy brother. ⁹ And Onan knew*

Fragrance Haters

that the seed should not be his; and it came to pass, when he went in unto his brother's wife, that he spilled it on the ground, lest that he should give seed to his brother. ¹⁰ *And the thing which he did displeased the LORD: wherefore he slew him also.*

Genesis 38:6-10

The verses above give us a little insight into Er's personality and his religious beliefs. Verse seven says he was wicked. The word wicked denotes being ungodly, evil, unrighteous and malignant. Wickedness is inspired by Satan and is also the spirit of anti-Christ. Since Er was wicked he operated in the spirit of anti-Christ; he was anti-procreation and anti-reproduction, therefore God killed him. Er did not want to see Tamar fulfilling God's plan for her life. Modern day Tamar's are hooking up men like Er who hate the plan of God and hate the woman they are with. The modern day Er may give you children but no commitment, no love, no marriage and no peace. Why would he do that? He is an anti-Christ.

The spirit of the Anti-Christ is not waiting to come into the world it is already here and has been in operation since the fall of man and continues to operate in people today. Men like Er just want to live life their way or they don't want to live at all. The Bible warns us not to be unequally yoked together with unbelievers because of their ungodly lifestyles.

*Little children, it is the last time: and as ye have heard that antichrist shall come, even **now are there many antichrists**; whereby we know that it is the last time.*

I John 2:18 (KJV)

¹ *Beloved, believe not every spirit, but try the spirits whether they are of God: because many false prophets are gone out into the world. 2 Hereby know ye the Spirit of God: Every spirit that confesseth that Jesus Christ is come in the flesh is of God:* ³ *And every spirit that confesseth*

131

Fragrance Haters

*not that Jesus Christ is come in the flesh is not of God: and this is that **spirit of antichrist**, whereof you have heard that it should come; and even **<u>now</u> already is it in the world**.*

I John 4:1-3 (KJV)

After Er's death Judah gave Tamar to his second son named Onan. Now Onan had a true hater spirit because he got pleasure from Tamar but wasted his seed on the ground instead of leaving it in Tamar's womb. The modern day Onan loves the pleasure of being with a woman physically but does not care about her. The spirit of Onan is why prostitution is so popular and will never go out of business because they are not interested in a committed relationship. He only wants to get his and that is all. Onan received this spirit from his father Judah, who after his wife died went out of town and hired a prostitute not knowing it was Tamar (Genesis 38:13-26). Onan basically treated Tamar like a prostitute and nothing more. He did not care about providing for her needs even though his name means wealthy. He hated her. How can he hate her and still have sex with her? Men do not need attraction, feelings or emotions to have sex; all they need is a woman. Stop thinking he is showing how much he cares by making love to you. When the sex is over and yet still no marriage, you are hated. Onan's selfish attitude displeased the Lord so God killed him also.

How Do Men Deal with Fragrance Haters?

Sometimes men will deal with fragrance haters themselves, especially if the woman involved is a wife or sister. No man wants his wife, daughter, mother, aunt, sister or any other significant woman in his life to be mishandled, mistreated, and mistaken to be easy like a prostitute. A man will do some serious damage to anyone who would do such a thing to the woman they love and hold in honor.

I have two brothers and one beautiful sister. Growing up my dad trained us boys to take care of our sister. He was always drilling it into our heads "Watch out for your sister". I tried to protect her from fragrance haters. I didn't want my sister to become one of the women that men sit around and

132

Fragrance Haters

laugh about and call only when they have an urge to use a woman (you know what I mean).

Genesis chapter 34 tells the story of Dinah, Jacob and Leah's daughter. Jacob's caravan was traveling through the land of Succoth where he built a house and came to Shalem, a city of Shechem in the land of Canaan. Dinah went out one day to watch the women of the land of Shalem and was taken up by the prince of that city named Shechem. He took Dinah and slept with her and fell in love with her. Shechem spoke well of Dinah and even asked her family for her hand in marriage. Dinah's brothers were offended and took action. They told Shechem "Yes you can marry Dinah but you must be circumcised first, you and all of your men". The day after the circumcisions Dinah's brothers knew they were sore and couldn't fight, so her brothers went in and killed them. The question is, how is Shechem a fragrance hater? He sounds like a nice man, but what you don't know is the background of Shechem. During recent excavations a decapitated donkey skeleton was found that appeared to be used for sacrifice. The donkey was seen as an unclean animal for sacrifice by the Israelites. Shechem's father was Hamor, whose name means "ass" in Hebrew. Shechem was the son of an ass and the whole city was named after the son of an ass (Shalem the city of asses). Shechem behaved stubbornly by unlawfully taking Dinah's virginity. He did things backwards by having sex with her first and then asking for her hand in marriage. The story is telling us that he was an ass because of his actions.

Tips for Christian Singles

- Work in the assignment God has given you (Genesis 2:18-20). Adam working for God as a single person is a good example.

- Don't wait for a husband before you begin to work for the Lord, work now!

- Develop your own financial foundation and strength.

- Invest in yourself, including: personal fitness, vacations, conferences, books, apparel, transportation, beauty care, etc.

- Practice holding meaningful conversations with people. This is where reading books on various topics, taking vacations and attending conferences can help you become well rounded and knowledgeable on many different topics.

- Practice listening. Communication is a two-way operation. You must be a good listener to give feedback and an accurate response to what was said.

- Become aware of the types of fruit you bear until all nine fruits of the Spirit are easily seen (Matthew 12:33).

- Seek God for spiritual gifts until they become seen and experienced by those around you (I Corinthians 14:1).

I Smell Jesus

Have you ever been around praying people who love the Lord and have given themselves totally to Jesus? Their presence is absolutely wonderful. Without question you know they have a connection with Jesus and can be trusted. You can just sense it, you can feel it and you can smell it. I remember when I first got saved I used to pray with the mothers of the church, sometimes shutting in and praying all night. I remember during those days of prayer a smell would come into my spirit making me so comfortable that I became sleepy. I cannot explain how I was able to smell in my spirit but I do know it brought me into a trance-like state. It was in this state that the Lord would speak to me. Whenever I read about how God caused a sleep to come upon Adam (Genesis 2:21), Abram (Genesis 15:12) and Peter (Acts 10:10 and 11:5) I wondered if God used a spiritual smell to put them to sleep or into a trance as He did me.

When I was in my early teens the call of God was heavy and strong on my life. Even though I did not accept the call right then, death could not take me out. I was in a devastating car accident and lived. The car was totaled. I was thrown half out of the window while the other three riders where thrown completely from the car, yet they didn't have a scratch on them. I was halfway in the car and half out while it was flipping. That was somewhat like my heart towards the Lord and the world "half in and half out". I was being tossed around not having any control over anything, not even my life or my death. What took only seconds seemed like hours to me as it happened in slow motion. I still remember seeing my head and

Fragrance Haters

body about to slam into the ground, but when I actually hit it even at great force I felt nothing. I could only think about how God was calling me and how I was running from Him. I remembered that two weeks prior to the accident a visiting prophet called my mother to the altar. He told her someone close to you will get into a bad car accident but don't worry the Lord will spare them. Yes, that was me; the Lord graciously spared my life just as He said.

From that point on I believed in the Prophetic Voice of God speaking through men. A few months after the car accident a minister from my church brought a prophet from New Orleans to our home. He was known to be a man of great prayer. When he came into the house he prayed and blessed our home and talked about the time he smelled Jesus in his prayer room. It blew me away. I was mesmerized by his story and had never heard anyone talk about smelling Jesus. I was 16 and very curious about the things of God. I asked the prophet, "What did Jesus smell like?" He said Jesus was sweet, like sweet smelling cologne. I then asked the prophet, "Why did Jesus allow you to smell Him?" He said, "Because I pray". What a wonderful blessing to have smelled Jesus. Nineteen years later I still have not forgotten about that prophet being privileged and blessed enough to smell the Lord in his prayer room. I have not experienced that privilege yet but His aroma is in my spirit. The Bible lets us know how Jesus smelled.

> *⁶Thy throne, O God, is for ever and ever: the sceptre of thy kingdom is a right sceptre. ⁷ Thou lovest righteousness, and hatest wickedness: therefore God, thy God, hath anointed thee with the oil of gladness above thy fellows. ⁸ All thy garments **smell of myrrh, and aloes, and cassia,** out of the ivory palaces, whereby they have made thee glad.*
>
> *Psalm 45:6-8 (KJV)*

Jesus smelled of three spices: myrrh, aloe and cassia. All three of these are very sweet smelling and have an association with wood. Jesus was anointed by God the Father and given a scepter, which is a symbol of authority. The scepter was given because of His righteousness and hatred

135

Fragrance Haters

of evil. This reveals the two ways to become anointed: (1) living a righteous life, and (2) hating all forms of evil. If you are going to receive a full outpouring of the anointed oil then you must become a lover of righteousness and absolutely hate all forms of evil, which includes certain movies and music. I'm not saying watching movies and listening to secular music is a sin, but they can stir up your flesh and emotions with suggestive lyrics and romantic scenes, so be mindful of what you allow yourself to partake in.

Anointed to Spread the Fragrance of Good News

> *[14] But thanks be to God, who made us his captives and leads us along in Christ's triumphal procession. Now wherever we go he uses us to tell others about the Lord and to spread the Good News like a sweet perfume. [15] Our lives are a fragrance presented by Christ to God. But this fragrance is perceived differently by those being saved and by those perishing. [16] To those who are perishing we are a fearful smell of death and doom. But to those who are being saved we are a life-giving perfume. And who is adequate for such a task as this?*

> *2 Corinthians 2:14-16 (New Living Translation)*

When we as the redeemed of the Lord open our mouths and spread the Word of God to those around us we are being used to spread His perfume. It must be refreshing to those who are in darkness to **see** some light. It has to delight the **taste buds** of those who have gone through life without salt to finally experience it; Jesus said you are the salt of the earth (Matthew 5:13). It must be comforting to have someone **touch** you with the finger of God after being handled by men. It must be good to finally **hear** the truth when all you have heard was lies. It must be wonderful to **smell** perfume instead of the stench of sin.

We are blessed with the honor of wearing the aroma of good news from heaven so people everywhere can smell what heaven is cooking. God has blessings stored up for people in the world but they cannot have them until

Fragrance Haters

we spread the aroma around by the life we live, the words we speak and the places we go. People are hurting, dying and searching for the aroma of LIFE that we have taken for granted. They will gamble way their futures to have what we have, to hear what we hear and to experience what we experience. They stay out all night for several days looking for what you have but they cannot find it doing the things they do. We must guide them to the Way, the Truth and the Life with the highly fragrant gospel of Jesus Christ.

Chapter 12

Leave Something for Him to Desire

[12] The king is lying on his couch, enchanted by the fragrance of my perfume. [13] My lover is like a sachet of myrrh lying between my breasts. [14] He is like a bouquet of flowers in the gardens of En-gedi.

Song of Solomon 1:12-14 (New Living Translation)

So many women make the mistake of thinking all a man wants is sex, and guess what? They give him some. Big mistake!! If a man sees you as a potential wife his expectations are high. He is obviously attracted to you, desires to be close and intimate but wants to get to know you first. He has set in his heart to wait because you just may be the one. He wants to find out what kind of woman you are. Do you have a sense of humor? What is your favorite food, flower, day of the week, etc? Where did you come from? Where have you been? Before he can seek answers he finds himself getting sex from you early on and now he is disappointed and doesn't need to ask any questions because he already has his answer.

The Shulammite woman knew she had the interest of the king just as much as she was interested in him. She said he was like myrrh lying between her breasts and wore a small pouch of the fragrance to remind her of him. Then she said the king was on his couch thinking of her and remembering the smell of her perfume. They were not only interested in getting to know each other but also wanted to be together in a sexual way, yet she did not put herself in a compromising situation. Let us face the facts of humanity; we all have natural feelings and desires. We are attracted to the opposite sex just the way God planned, yet He commands us to restrain our feelings until we are married. It is not evil or sinful to

Leave Something for Him to Desire

have these feelings, but it is wrong to act upon them in an unlawful way. Sexual feelings are a blessing from God but having sex outside of the marriage covenant is against God's plan and it is a sin against your own body.

I truly feel most people, whether they are saved and in the church or lost in the world, have a conversation disorder. They simply run out of things to talk about, become bored and then are willing to enter into the physical part of the relationship.

Christians who date should do so around other people who can hold you accountable for your actions and help keep you in line. Parents who send their teenagers out on dates with other teens that have raging sexual hormones, without supervision, and expect them to be ok are not wise. I offer the same advice for Christian adults. I must admit it is more difficult to counsel adults because they feel they should be able to go out by themselves and spend time alone in each others' homes, even staying overnight (in separate rooms – so they say). I have seen instances of dating couples that have gotten auto loans, opened joint bank accounts, adopted children, taken vacations to far away places staying in the same room and finally moved in together to save money for the wedding. They also spend excessive amounts of time with the boyfriend/girlfriend's child or children; all of this while first of all declaring to be a Christian, and secondly not yet married. The sad thing is most of the couples that make these poor decisions never marry or if they do the marriage ends quickly.

Many people get saved without seeking to learn how to truly live the new life according to the Spirit of the Lord. The new life in the Spirit is developed through time in a process called Transformation.

> [1] *I beseech you therefore, brethren, by the mercies of God, that ye present your bodies a living sacrifice, holy, acceptable unto God, which is your reasonable service.* [2] *And be not conformed to this world: but be ye **transformed by the renewing of your mind**, that ye may prove what is that good, and acceptable, and perfect, will of God.*

Leave Something for Him to Desire

Romans 12:1-2 (KJV)

The transformation process is simply replacing the old worldly way of thinking, living and reacting with the Word of God. To guarantee the transformation takes place you must be in a place where you can hear the Word taught and preached. Dating without receiving Bible-based instructions from your spiritual leaders will ensure that you end up doing exactly what you've always done in past relationships. So many people receive Jesus as Lord and still live their lives the same way as before they got saved. They are adults in the natural sense without realizing they are babies in the spirit. They must be taught how to live in the spirit, walk in the spirit and most importantly please the Spirit of the Lord.

The Odor of Decay

> And when the sabbath was past, Mary Magdalene, and Mary the mother of James, and Salome, had bought sweet spices, that they might come and anoint him.

Mark 16:1 (KJV)

Embalming the dead was not part of the Jewish custom; they did not place anything inside the deceased body, but instead applied spices to the outside. They used sweet spices to cover the stench of death. The pouring on of sweet spices was also a gesture of love and devotion. The women brought their spices to the tomb ready to cover Jesus, but when they arrived to their surprise He had risen. It was not necessary for them to anoint Him but He needed to anoint them with His fragrance. He said, "I go unto my Father and He shall send you the Comforter, the Holy Ghost" (John 14:16). How was the Comforter to come? He was to be poured out just like perfumed oil (Joel 2:28).

When Adam sinned death was released upon all flesh (mankind). On the other hand life is given to everyone who believes in Jesus the Son of God who takes away the sin of the world. God anoints the believer with the fragrance of Jesus so He will not be insulted by your decaying human odor (mistakes, failures, fears, doubts, sickness, weaknesses and sin). The Lord

Leave Something for Him to Desire

desires to smell the aroma of His Son Jesus, the one who pleased God so much He shouted it from the heavens to the earth on more than one occasion, saying "This is my beloved Son, in whom I am well pleased" (Matthew 3:17 and 17:5). God does the same for us throughout the universe and the earth. Whenever God speaks about us His favor begins to knock down walls and move mountains; things start to work for you instead of against you. His favor speaks to kingdoms and nations on our behalf, providing opportunities and opening doors. This favor will cause people to give to you and speak well of you, without even knowing who you are. This pleasing aroma will cause men to come where you are and ask for your hand in marriage.

"Love covers a multitude of sins" (I Peter 4:8). This is exactly what the love of God has done for us. He loved us so much He covered our countless sins by not remembering them and placing the favorable fragrance of His Son on us. Whenever He desires to enjoy the fragrance of someone on earth He reaches down and smells one of His anointed ones, saying this is my beloved son or daughter in whom I am well pleased.

Chapter 13

Catfish (What is that smell?)

*Then the LORD said to Moses and Aaron, ² "Give the following instructions to the Israelites: The animals you may use for food ³ include those that have completely divided hooves and chew the cud. ⁴ You may not, however, eat the animals named here because they either have split hooves or chew the cud, but not both. The camel may not be eaten, for though it chews the cud, it does not have split hooves. ⁵ The same is true of the rock badger ⁶ and the hare, so they also may never be eaten. ⁷ And the pig may not be eaten, for though it has split hooves, it does not chew the cud. ⁸ You may not eat the meat of these animals or touch their dead bodies. They are ceremonially unclean for you. ⁹ "As for marine animals, you may eat whatever has **both fins and scales**, whether taken from fresh water or salt water. ¹⁰ You may not, however, eat marine animals that do not have both fins and scales. You are to detest them, ¹¹ and they will always be forbidden to you. You must never eat their meat or even touch their dead bodies. ¹² I repeat, __any marine animal that does not have both fins and scales is strictly forbidden to you__.*

Leviticus 11:1-12 (New Living Translation)

The heading is "Catfish", but don't let it scare you off. It is not my intention to insinuate you smell like catfish, but instead I want to talk about the nature of catfish. The scriptures above are very interesting, especially in verses nine through twelve in relation to clean and unclean fish. I will relate these verses to attracting the right man into your life.

142

Catfish (What is that smell?)

Ever so often I break out the fishing pole from the garage and go with some of the Deacons and brothers in the church just to hang out. I don't really like fishing because two elements are needed that I just don't want to use: faith and patience. Fishing poses a problem for me because I want to visibly see if any fish are available. If I can't see any fish beyond the muddy water it makes me want to take my pole and leave. If I could just see them in the water it would encourage me to continue, but most of the time I can only have faith they will be attracted to my bait and take a bite.

You must be the same way when it comes to waiting on the Lord to send the man of God into your life. Know the aroma of your spirit is anointed by Jesus to draw your husband in. A lot of sisters become discouraged because they cannot see what they've been searching for. You may not be able to see the good men come anywhere near you, but God is faithful.

The prophet Elijah called the nation of Israel to Mount Carmel for a showdown against the false prophets of Baal. Shortly after defeating the false prophets and killing them, Jezebel came into religious power. Every true prophet of God that she could find was killed. Elijah thought he was the only one left.

> *²² Then Elijah said to them, "I am the only prophet of the LORD who is left, but Baal has 450 prophets.*
>
> *I Kings 18:22 (New Living Translation)*

Although there seemed to be no real prophets left, God had a reserve hidden from the human eye. Elijah fled from the presence of Jezebel because she threatened to have him murdered. He ran for his life and was severely depressed and a little suicidal. When he finally arrived to a certain place God met him and asked "What are you doing Elijah?" He responded by saying:

> *¹⁴ "I have zealously served the LORD God Almighty. But the people of Israel have broken their covenant with you, torn down your altars, and killed every one of your prophets. **I alone am left**, and now they are trying to kill*

143

Catfish (What is that smell?)

me, too."

I Kings 19:14 (New Living Translation)

God's response to Elijah was "It looks like there are no more. I know you think you are by yourself but I am God and I will always have someone to do My works". You must know God will provide. He always has somewhere in the wings and when it is time He will bring them out of waiting into the place He has purposed for them.

> *[18] Yet I have left me **seven thousand** in Israel, all the knees which have not bowed unto Baal, and every mouth which hath not kissed him.*
>
> *I Kings 19:18 (KJV)*

As you can see God is never without a reserve, a small group of people that will not give in to the pressures of the world's system. He will always have a supply available to meet the needs of those who serve Him. "But my God shall supply all your need according to His riches in glory by Christ Jesus" (Philippians 4:19). Put on the Spiritual Scent of the Lord and hold your head up. What has been reserved is set aside for your pleasure, for your enjoyment and **no good thing will He withhold** from them who walk uprightly (Psalm 84:11).

Countless potential husbands have been reserved by God for women like you; women who are anointed with the fragrance of salvation and will keep their fragrance pure and holy. All the shameless women that repeatedly disrespect their bodies cannot touch what's been reserved for you by God. The prisons cannot lock up what's been reserved for you by God. The homosexuals cannot pervert what's been reserved for you by God. The devil cannot possess what's been reserved for you by God. Premature death cannot take what's been reserved for you by God. My sister, be encouraged, even when you can't see potential husbands around. We walk by faith and not by sight (II Corinthians 5:7)

Besides not seeing the fish, I mentioned hating to use patience when going fishing. Even after discovering there are actually fish in the water I really don't like that the fish haven't bit the bait on my pole. Why should I have

Catfish (What is that smell?)

to wait when the fish are there? Get on the pole! Get on the pole! Bite the bait! Bite it! What's wrong with you fish? Aren't you hungry? Impatient fishers are always reeling in their bait and hook to check and see if any fish have nibbled (that's what I do), not realizing the longer that bait stays fixed in one place the more likely it is for the fish to pick up the scent and be drawn to it. You must stay put. Stop running all over the place from church to church and home to home like a chicken with its head cut off. Tell yourself to **stand still** and see the salvation (deliverance) of the Lord (Exodus 14:13). It is better to be consistent in what you do and where you go so they can locate your aroma. Most churches are filled with sisters who love the Lord, who are living right, and yes, want to be married. It gets to be really overwhelming for the sisters who start to look around the church only to find the few men who are there are either already married and off limits, married and cheating (no good), single but gay, single but sleeping with half the women in the church, single but crazy and lazy, and/or single but too old. Stay put and watch God perform His word.

Bottom Feeders

Catfish are notorious bottom feeders, spending their lives eating discarded things that have fallen to the bottom, which is why God forbade His people to eat such unclean things. Bottom feeders are full of bad cholesterol; this includes crabs, shrimp and lobsters, all of which elevate the blood pressure and can lead to heart disease. Catfish live their lives at the bottom of dirty murky waters where darkness prevails with very small amounts of light. While they swim around at the bottom these unclean fish suck on mud, sand, dead fish, rocks, shells, bones, bottles, trash, used hypodermic needles, cans, and all other kinds of garbage.

It is my observation that broken, cut, disassembled, destroyed and dead objects will often fall to the bottom. Things that were at one time alive, thriving and growing are now dead and have become the catfish's favorite food, which happens to be dead, rotten and stinky things. They get excited over funk and death because if it were not for the dead they would not eat. They are catfish. Everything that lies on the bottom eats from the bottom, plays and dwells on the bottom and is cursed to be there. Bottom feeders are cursed by God.

Catfish (What is that smell?)

And the LORD *God said unto the serpent, Because thou hast done this, thou art cursed above all cattle, and above every beast of the field; upon thy belly shalt thou go, and* **dust shalt thou eat all the days of thy life**.

Genesis 3:14 (KJV)

The nature and activity of catfish remind me of the spiritual nature of some people; they are low down, cold-blooded, cold hearted, sneaky, conniving liars. Don't get mad at the natural catfish, but the **spiritual catfish** are the ones that need some prayer. They don't care about anything or anyone else as long as they can get what they want. It doesn't matter if the person they want is married, saved or engaged. Low down is not just a term we should use on the people who appear on scandalous talk shows. Prominent people like school teachers, coaches, principles, lawyers, doctors, pastors, Sunday school teachers, uncles, aunts, mothers, fathers, wives, brothers, sisters, husbands, friends -- you name it, can be low down as well; and even more so because they use relationships, titles, positions of power and influence to get what they want.

These catfish people are low down and dirty. They are out to get theirs, not caring about the feelings of others. Like catfish, some people love dark places and are driven by their own selfish lusts. They say hurtful and harmful things. They sow seeds of discord so they can move in on the bait. They can sense the slightest scent of death and decay on a weak woman or weak man so they can land in bed with them. They can smell when a marriage is dead or dying and move in on the man or the woman wearing the odor of an upcoming divorce. It doesn't surprise me to find out some people's best friend end up in bed with their husband or wife. I have counseled many people through this experience; some were even in the church. Don't be surprised but catfish can even be relatives. God is warning us that you cannot put anything past a catfish; they are untrustworthy creatures of the dark. Catfish can smell when you are trying hard to put the alcohol away but will come around and offer you a free drink. They can even be in your local church, which is why Jesus warned us to watch and pray (Mark 14:38). Be prayerful and on the alert for these prowlers.

Catfish (What is that smell?)

Catfish are basically blind. Their eyes are very dim so they use their whiskers to feel around through the dark. That's exactly how unsaved and unclean people go through life. They move according to what they feel which is how they end up in so much trouble. The righteous, however "walk by faith and not by sight" (II Corinthians 5:7). Catfish really depend on their keen sense of smell. They can smell flesh decaying even in water. If something stinks in the water the catfish will find it and devour it. Only blind people will do some of the dirty things that they do. Only the blind will step into some of the things that they step into. Are you surprised to learn catfish cannot see? I didn't think you were.

> *But he that hateth his brother is in darkness, and walketh in darkness, and knoweth not whither he goeth, because that darkness hath blinded his eyes.*

> *I John 2:11 (KJV)*

> *In whom the god of this world hath blinded the minds of them which believe not, lest the light of the glorious gospel of Christ, who is the image of God, should shine unto them.*
> *II Corinthians 4:4 (KJV)*

Fins and Scales

God makes a distinctive difference between fish with both fins and scales and fish that lack both. The fish with fins and scales were considered clean and good to eat but the fish without both were unclean, detestable and not to be eaten.

Fins help to further mobility within the fish's environment (water). Lots of unclean fish have fins but lack scales, which is to say they have a religious system. They have designed their own way to worship God, just like other false worshippers but the religious system has not produced a higher moral standard or a connection to God. Their fins have not produced a higher way of thinking and living. They follow false religions and occult practices like horoscopes, astrology, fortune telling, tarot cards,

147

Catfish (What is that smell?)

Buddhism, Hinduism, Islam, Ritualism, etc. Neither has their fake religion produced scales. Scales provide an outer covering of protection from the environmental elements. Fish with scales can swim in the same water as a catfish and never behave nor eat like a catfish. Jesus' prayer for every believer said:

> [14] *I have given them thy word; and the world hath hated them, because they are not of the world, even as I am not of the world.* [15] *I pray not that thou shouldest take them out of the world, but that thou shouldest keep them from the evil.* [16] *They are not of the world, even as I am not of the world.* [17] *Sanctify them through thy truth: thy word is truth.* [18] *As thou hast sent me into the world, even so have I also sent them into the world.* [19] *And for their sakes I sanctify myself, that they also might be sanctified through the truth.* [20] *Neither pray I for these alone, but for them also which shall believe on me through their word;*
>
> *John 17:14-20 (KJV)*

Beloved we are the fish with scales. We have been sanctified and set aside as clean in an unclean world. The world is dirty but we are not. The world is evil but we are not. The world hates Jesus but we love Him. The world is full of catfish without scales and filthy moral habits. We are in the world but our scales protect us from the filth of the world. The scales help to guard our hearts, minds and bodies. The scales are a symbol of receiving the baptism in the Holy Ghost because the Holy Ghost is not only inside us but upon us. He has been poured out on us. Notice the following scriptures on how the Spirit will be upon us.

> *And it shall come to pass afterward, that I will pour out my spirit **upon all flesh**; and your sons and your daughters shall prophesy, your old men shall dream dreams, your young men shall see visions:*
>
> *Joel 2:28 (KJV)*

148

Catfish (What is that smell?)

*But ye shall receive power, after that the **Holy Ghost is come upon you**: and ye shall be witnesses unto me both in Jerusalem, and in all Judea, and in Samaria, and unto the uttermost part of the earth.*

Acts 1:8 (KJV)

[16] And Jesus, when he was baptized, went up straightway out of the water: and, lo, the heavens were opened unto him, and he saw the Spirit of God descending like a dove, and lighting upon him:

Matthew 3:16 (KJV)

If you don't know what kind of fish you want let me tell you what kind you need. You need a fish with fins and scales. You need a man who is able to move with his fins (faith) and one who has received the baptism of scales (the Holy Ghost). A man of Faith and the Holy Ghost is the same description of the type of men the Apostles were seeking to assist them in kingdom work, and they found seven. I want you to know your clean Spiritual Fragrance will draw fish with fins and scales to you.

*[3] Wherefore, brethren, look ye out among you seven **men of honest report**, **full of the Holy Ghost** and wisdom, whom we may appoint over this business. [4] But we will give ourselves continually to prayer, and to the ministry of the word. [5] And the saying pleased the whole multitude: and they chose Stephen, a man full of **faith** and of the **Holy Ghost**, and Philip, and Prochorus, and Nicanor, and Timon, and Parmenas, and Nicolas a proselyte of Antioch:*

Acts 6:3-5 (KJV)

Stingrays and catfish get stepped on because they don't have scales. Fish without scales are not as sensitive to movement in the water. On any given summer day on many beaches you are likely to find someone has stepped on a stingray which is a very painful experience. This happened to the unaware beachgoer all because the stingray didn't have scales and could not feel danger coming. So it is with the catfish, it has no scales and

Catfish (What is that smell?)

cannot feel what is happening in its environment. The stingray and the catfish are natural examples of a spiritual reality. They paint a picture of how unsaved people live life without concern for what God is saying or doing. They don't care they just want to get theirs. Their attitude is, so what if there is an after life and a judgment and the wrath of God; I want to live by my rules, it's my prerogative. Catfish. Are you a catfish? Do you date catfish? I pray not, but if you are, you should ask God for a new nature and for Him to fill and baptize you with His Spirit.

People who live their lives like catfish are morally and spiritually unclean because they lack scales. Consequently they cannot feel or comprehend what is happening in the spirit realm. Fish without scales cannot tell when trouble or judgment is coming. When the Spirit of the Lord is moving they don't know it. When the Word of the Lord is proclaimed to fish with scales they can feel the Word in the spirit realm, they can hear the Word in the spirit realm and they can perceive the Word in the spirit realm, all so they can receive it in the natural realm. Thus they obey God and receive His blessing and avoid the danger of judgment.

Whales are not considered fish but they are also unclean because they lack scales. A whale in Hebrew is **Tan**. Tan/Tannin means "sea-monster" or "dragon". The whale or the shark (also without scales) was the great fish that swallowed Jonah (Jonah 1:17) and held him for three days. It was considered untamable like the waves of the sea (Job 7:12). The whale is a biblical symbol of Satan or a powerful principality. Read what Ezekiel says about Pharaoh who is a biblical symbol of Satan as well. Ezekiel was given the mandate to prophecy in the form of a poem that was accompanied by crying. This style of prophecy was used to announce calamity and it was called a lamentation.

> [2] Son of man, take up a lamentation for Pharaoh king of Egypt, and say unto him, Thou art like a young lion of the nations, and thou art as a **whale** in the seas: and thou camest forth with thy rivers, and troubledst the waters with thy feet, and fouledst their rivers. [3] Thus saith the Lord GOD; I will therefore spread out my net over thee with a company of many people; and they shall bring thee up in

Catfish (What is that smell?)

my net. [4] Then will I leave thee upon the land, I will cast thee forth upon the open field, and will cause all the fowls of the heaven to remain upon thee, and I will fill the beasts of the whole earth with thee. [5] And I will lay thy flesh upon the mountains, and fill the valleys with thy height. [6] I will also water with thy blood the land wherein thou swimmest, even to the mountains; and the rivers shall be full of thee. [7] And when I shall put thee out, I will cover the heaven, and make the stars thereof dark; I will cover the sun with a cloud, and the moon shall not give her light. [8] All the bright lights of heaven will I make dark over thee, and set darkness upon thy land, saith the Lord GOD.

Ezekiel 32:2-8 (KJV)

Fish with scales are very good for the cardiovascular system, heart, brain, hair, skin and so many other body parts because they are high in good cholesterol. So are good men, they will not break your heart with selfish deeds but instead will add to your life. Fish without scales (the unsaved and uncommitted) have bad cholesterol but fish with scales (the saved and committed) have good cholesterol. Unholy men break the hearts of women and shorten life spans with their evil ways. You should be waiting patiently for fish with scales; they are good for your spiritual health.

In order to catch fish with scales you have to set your line up higher in the water, which is to say raise your life up to the next level. You must have a highly fragrant anointing to catch such a fish. You should be soaked in the fragrance of the Lord to bring these fish to you. You cannot catch a good stripper or perch at the bottom of the lake; neither can you draw a good man if you have bad morals. Look for desirable fish in higher places like the church, Christian functions, weddings, schools, prayer meetings, etc. Avoid catfish dens like nightclubs, house parties, bars, places where drugs and alcohol are used, pre-marital sexual relations, and privacy with men in closed spaces or alone where no one else is around. The Spiritually Perfumed Woman must avoid places like these. I know you are an adult but I am a spiritual father; I am warning you catfish are ruthless. You could become pregnant, diseased or worse (you can lose the fragrance of

Catfish (What is that smell?)

the LORD). Stay away from catfish.

Things to look for in a good man (fish)

- **Is he a true Christian?**
  Or did he just confess Christ and still leads a sinful life?

- **Is he a man of his word?**
  If he can't keep his word does he avoid you or does he take responsibility and explain why?

- **Is he committed to a church?**
  Or does he sacrifice worship time to instead spend with friends, etc?

- **Does he show respect to spiritual leadership?**

- **Is he committed to a job?**
  Has he worked at his job for a considerable amount of time or does he jump from place to place?

- **Does he ask you for sex?**
  If so he is not the one (a man who is thinking about marriage won't go for that).

- **Is he accountable?**
  Can he say where he has been without getting upset or lying to you?

- **Does he have a good temperament?**
  Are his emotions under control or does he fly off the handle when things don't go his way?

- **Does he live by the Word of God?**
  If he does not read the Bible he cannot live by the Bible.

Catfish (What is that smell?)

Test Your Spiritual Fragrance

1. List nine reasons why odor and smell are important on earth.

   _____   _____   _____
   _____   _____   _____
   _____   _____   _____

2. List two virtues you need to catch a fish.

   _____   _____

3. How many men did God tell Elijah were reserved?

4. What does it mean to be a bottom feeder?

5. The whale is a prophetic picture of:
   a. Angels   b. Satan   c. People

6. Write a small paragraph on the purpose and importance of scales.

7. What is the spiritual significance of fins?

8. Name some catfish behavior.

9. What types of bait do fish with scales look for?

10. Where do fish with scales swim? Top or Bottom (circle one)

Chapter 14

Why Do the Bad Ones Keep Coming to You?

When an evil spirit leaves a person, it goes into the desert, searching for rest. But when it finds none, it says, 'I will return to the person I came from'.

Luke 11:24 (New Living Translation)

*L*ooking for something to tear up!

When an unclean spirit leaves a person it walks around in dry places searching for rest. Two words from the quoted scripture are important for us to examine closely. The first is desert (dry places) and the other is rest. The word "desert" or "dry places" in Greek is *Anudros,* meaning "waterless" or to be "without water".

Anudros = Waterless

Before we explore the waterless, let's talk briefly about the watered. Woman of God you are watered by God because you believe in Jesus Christ the Son of God. The day you became a believer is the day Jesus placed a spring of water inside, giving life to you and those around you. The water in you has the power of current (force) that moves everything in its path out of the way. That same current, that river, is what the enemy is trying to damn up like a beaver, because he knows if you begin to use your river his kingdom is in serious trouble. Jesus said:

> *[37] If you are thirsty, come to me! [38] If you believe in me, come and drink! For the Scriptures declare that rivers of living water will flow out from within. [39] (When he said "living water," he was speaking of the Spirit, who would*

Why Do the Bad Ones Keep Coming to You?

> *be given to everyone believing in him. But the Spirit had not yet been given, because Jesus had not yet entered into his glory.)*
>
> *John 7:37-39 (New Living Translation)*

You are a well-watered garden; better than any tropical forest, yielding beautiful and precious fruit. You are the Paradise of the Lord; attractive and of very high value because of the living water inside you. Jesus told Nicodemus:

> *Verily, verily; I say unto thee, Except a man be born of water and of the Spirit, he cannot enter into the kingdom of God. [6] That which is born of the flesh is flesh; and that which is born of the Spirit is spirit.*
>
> *John 3:5-6 (KJV)*

Isn't it interesting that while Jesus was being baptized in the Jordan River (a body of water) Satan was not there, but instead Satan tempted Jesus in the wilderness (dry places)? That is exactly where the enemy desires to meet you.

The desert places, *anudros,* are people who have never given their lives to Jesus and are not saved. They are dry bones. Waterless people are the property of Satan, the god of this world, of whom unclean spirits and demons have the right to them, at will. You must identify them and keep them away from your water; unless you are sharing the water of life by proclaiming the word of God, guard it with all diligence.

Unclean spirits have open access to waterless people but do not delight in influencing them alone. Demonic spirits have a destructive mentality and love to demolish anything good, clean and watered by the Lord. They want to spoil your fragrance from the Lord and cause it to stink. They would love for your prayers to stink and not be answered, for your praise to stink and ultimately your entire life to stink.

The day you gave your life to Jesus you were swept of all evil spirits, cleansed and put in proper order so He could dwell in your heart as the

Why Do the Bad Ones Keep Coming to You?

Lord of your life. Let me tell you, there is nothing more attractive to a man seriously searching for a wife than to find a woman whose inward parts are washed clean and priorities are in place. That tells him you are serious about serving Jesus and that you have room for him at the top of your priorities. No man wants to go into a marriage not having his wife's attention because her priorities are backward; she doesn't know how to pay bills or keep a house in order, and is emotionally out of control.

Most men that are interested in you will come and check you out. Some are coming to see how far you are willing to go and yes, they will go the distance if you let them. Just know if you let them go the distance they are thinking "This woman is easy so I can't trust her. How many others have been here and done the same?" Jesus compares the person whom the spirits came out of to a house that was swept clean. When the dismissed spirit became bored in the waterless place he came back to where he used to call home and found it cleaned and in order. Once you get your house cleaned you need a strong man (Jesus) to stand guard over it. Without the protection and covering of Jesus, you are leaving the front door of your house wide open for even worse trouble than before to enter in.

The next word from that scripture (Luke 11:24) is rest, or *anapausis* in Greek, which means "recreation". Spirits do not require physical rest because they are immortal beings, not hampered by the limitations of fleshly bodies as we are. The rest they seek is being able to "set up shop" in a permanent place where they can effect even more damage on earth through a physical body.

Anapausis = Recreation or Rest

Some men that come into your life are direct agents of Satan. They come to steal, kill and destroy. Most women are either totally unaware or choose to ignore a warning from the Spirit of the Lord. These agents of Satan don't give off a satanic aroma because they are charming, gentle, hard working, affectionate and thoughtful. With these few desirable traits, or less, they have enough to fool a good woman who is lonely and looking for a man. When men are drawn to your aroma be on your guard, ready to discern their spirit. If you are vulnerable, looking for sexual relief or

Why Do the Bad Ones Keep Coming to You?

seeking a friend to talk to, you may fall into the destructive plan of the devil. Avoid the ugly cycle of sexual abuse or sex outside of a marital commitment; it can bring a curse on both you and your children.

If you are struggling with these types of issues, let me give you some advice. If for whatever reason you cannot be spiritually discerning because you are love struck and not strong enough to make the right decision, then I suggest you surround yourself with Holy Ghost filled, spiritually gifted people. Commit your spiritual growth to them. Get under their authority, sit and be taught by them through the Word of God. When you fall into a really weak moment call and ask them to pray with you right then and there. Never miss a chance to go to church; to receive sound teaching, ministering in the spirit and the opportunity to be delivered, because you've got to be free... Now. Get around people who are truly committed to holy living and will tell you the truth, even if it hurts. This will help to protect your cleaned house. Find a mentor who can speak deliverance and healing into your life, with the authority of God's Word. Seek out a faithful, praying church mother. Commit yourself to attending the prayer hour at your local church and submit to spiritual authority. Finally, be willing to say yes when direction and instruction is given. All of this requires a complete change in mentality and serious commitment on your part, but ask yourself: "Am I worth it?"

Lust will look past you going to church, your Jesus pin, long dress and the Bible you carry. Lust is only interested in its fulfillment and when it recognizes a place in you that is ready and willing, it moves. You must be equipped with the power of the spirit of discernment to recognize the motives of the man attracted to you. The spirit of discernment will let you know what is going on in his heart. Is he serious about developing a relationship in the will of God or did he just come to sample your fragrance and move on? You need discernment because you cannot afford to be the victim of another man on the prowl. Too much joy is waiting ahead to give in to lust. Your future is too bright and too blessed to allow this cycle to continue.

Your destiny is calling you forward to the time and place where you will be loved, adored, protected and cherished by a man who has been

Why Do the Bad Ones Keep Coming to You?

developed by God. This is why you must be encouraged to keep your fragrance pure and undefiled. This is why you must be faithful and avoid making bad decisions when it comes to relationships, sex and dating. Mistakes distort your vision; they cover the road of destiny with mud and dirt until the hope is all gone. If that has been the case for you, please don't lose hope and think it is all over. The God we serve is a God of many chances. Know that mistakes can be major time wasters and serve as hindrances to walking into your destiny.

Do not be weary in well doing but watch and pray. Your job is to be faithful even though you maybe lonely and hurting. I speak prophetically to you: if you keep yourself in the love of God and your fragrance pure you **will** attract the interest of God's man (your future husband). Your love and marriage will be a lasting one that leaves a wonderful legacy of love, respect and honor for your children and your children's children to see, admire and follow after.

When the devil tempted Jesus in the wilderness and was unsuccessful, the Bible says he left Jesus for a season. He did not leave forever. Most of Satan's attacks were strategic in nature but he continued to reappear (John 14:30). The devil apparently thought the time was right to try Jesus again; but Jesus said the prince of this world has come to check me out hoping to find a way in, but he still cannot find one single place of darkness in me.

Every woman of God should aspire to respond to temptation just as Jesus did; whether you are being checked out by agents of Satan or by the man of God. I want you to know if the devil can find just a little room in you he will keep coming back until he gets a chance to tear you up. Have you ever seen a couch or chair with a small hole in it and over time that hole became larger? You never see who is responsible for making that hole worse, yet it continues to grow until the whole thing is ruined. That little hole catches the attention of small children, big children, adults and anyone else that notices it, touches it or pulls on it making it gradually bigger. That is the same way lustful spirits operate. When they see a hole in you they pull on the strings, touch it and probe it, hoping to destroy the entire person not just make the hole larger. That's right. They want to tear you into pieces.

Why Do the Bad Ones Keep Coming to You?

Lustful men will tear you up and satisfy your sexual surges to the point you will forget the good girl, the daughter, the mother you were. Once lust pulls you out of the plan of God and under its power you are in jeopardy of losing everything good because whenever lust is fulfilled it brings forth death (James 1:13-15). When lustful men see something in you that is open to them they will keep coming back until all of you is open.

When the deceiver came to Eve in the Garden of Eden, he soon realized she was open to his deceptive plan. He also knew he could not come to her in any form. He had to come in a deceptive form, something that looked good and sounded wise.

> *¹ Now the serpent was the shrewdest of all the creatures the LORD God had made. "Really?" he asked the woman. "Did God really say you must not eat any of the fruit in the garden?"*
>
> *² "Of course we may eat it," the woman told him. ³ "It's only the fruit from the tree at the center of the garden that we are not allowed to eat. God says we must not eat it or even touch it, or we will die."*
>
> *⁴ "You won't die!" the serpent hissed. ⁵ "God knows that your eyes will be opened when you eat it. You will become just like God, knowing everything, both good and evil."*
>
> *⁶ The woman was convinced. The fruit looked so fresh and delicious, and it would make her so wise! So she ate some of the fruit. She also gave some to her husband, who was with her. Then he ate it, too. ⁷ At that moment, their eyes were opened, and they suddenly felt shame at their nakedness. So they strung fig leaves together around their hips to cover themselves.*
>
> *Genesis 3:1-7 (New Living Translation)*

In Genesis 3:1 the Bible lets us know the serpent was more wise, shrewd,

Why Do the Bad Ones Keep Coming to You?

cunning and crafty than all of the creatures the Lord God made. Satan was that serpent. He was a fallen angel kicked out of heaven because of sinful pride in the wisdom, beauty and talents that God had given him. I find it very interesting that Satan decided to enter into the serpent to approach Eve.

> *[12] Thus saith the Lord GOD; Thou sealest up the sum, full of wisdom, and perfect in beauty. [13] Thou hast been in Eden the garden of God; every precious stone was thy covering, the sardius, topaz, and the diamond, the beryl, the onyx, and the jasper, the sapphire, the emerald, and the carbuncle, and gold: the workmanship of thy tabrets and of thy pipes was prepared in thee in the day that thou wast created. [14] Thou art the anointed cherub that covereth; and I have set thee so: thou wast upon the holy mountain of God; thou hast walked up and down in the midst of the stones of fire. [15] Thou wast perfect in thy ways from the day that thou wast created, till iniquity was found in thee. [16] By the multitude of thy merchandise they have filled the midst of thee with violence, and thou hast sinned: therefore I will cast thee as profane out of the mountain of God: and I will destroy thee, O covering cherub, from the midst of the stones of fire. [17] Thine heart was lifted up because of thy beauty, thou hast corrupted thy wisdom by reason of thy brightness.*
>
> *Ezekiel 28:12-17 (KJV)*

According to Ezekiel, Lucifer was a brilliant high-ranking angel. He was beautifully arrayed by God his creator, with diamonds and rubies of all colors built right into him. Sharp dressing pimps use their flashy style to help them catch the eye of a potential prostitute then hook her into their harem. Now, to me and every other sober minded person, pimps clothes are to be laughed at because they look like human peacocks or clowns who forgot the circus. Apparently a lot of stray woman are drawn to them like moths to a flame.

Doesn't that sound a lot like what Satan did to Eve? He came to her in the

Why Do the Bad Ones Keep Coming to You?

form of the wisest animal that looked good and spoke well (the serpent). Isn't that what some of these men are doing? Looking well and speaking well, looking the part but don't have a part at all, faking it and never making it. They only end up being a bad investment of your time. How did the devil know Eve was open to his deceptive approach? How does a man with evil intentions know you are open to his advances?

The first thing Satan noticed about Eve was her body language. It's pretty easy to tell when someone is unhappy, joyful, tired, confused, angry, agitated or unhealthy. All of these can be observed through a person's body language. Your body language says a lot to a man. This is why you must be open to the leading of the Spirit of God at all times. Take notice of your body language; what does it say? Does it say my body belongs to God and I am content to wait until the Lord sends me what I need? Or does it say I am hot and I'll get with you if you say the right thing? Men will read your body posture; the way you walk in front of them, the way you stand, the way you smile or laugh at their jokes, your head movement, and the type of eye contact you give. Men will read into a touch on their shoulder much more differently than you may have intended. They study the way you say hello or good-bye, looking for the slightest sign that says you want them.

Even married women sometimes give off the wrong signal with body language that is appealing to single men. When approached by the wrong man at the right time some inappropriate things could begin to happen; exchanging numbers, talking on the phone for long periods of time, going to lunch, then to dinner, thinking and dreaming of each other and finally committing the selfish act of betrayal (adultery).

Dress to Attract the Best

Be very careful of the type of clothes you wear. I have noticed first hand that clothing changes the way you feel, walk, talk and think. Clothes can make you look and feel younger or make you look tired and old. They can also make you look and feel rich or poor. The way your dress can also make you look like a potential wife or an easy target for a one-night stand.

161

Why Do the Bad Ones Keep Coming to You?

You may be a good woman walking in true holiness but you could be misread by a good man who is genuinely interested in you or by some thug who just wants a piece of you. The good man may see your body language and dress ethics and walk away but a thug most likely will stick around to see what you are offering.

Beginning in elementary school, young girls are under pressure to reveal more flesh to get the boys attention and show off to other girls. Now the schools are forced to send the girls home to change into more appropriate clothing because they are so under dressed. I hear brothers in the barber shop or the gym talking about the young girls whose bodies look mature yet they are only thirteen; wearing low cut jeans, mini skirts and tiny snug-fitting shirts that are so revealing it leaves very little for the man's imagination and more importantly opens the door to lust. When men see a woman in revealing clothes they come to the immediate conclusion she is easy and willing to take the next step. That's right, sex.

Have you ever seen women wearing leotards or body-hugging workout clothes at the gym? When I see women wearing those things I feel a sense of sadness because instead of seeing them as the other men do (she is easy, looking for attention) I see them as confused and hurting. Maybe they are seeking attention from men but they get the wrong kind. When women wear very revealing clothing it is an obvious sign to a man they are begging for his attention sexually, which may not be the case. I am only trying to help you see how men think. I personally believe a woman wearing a leotard in a public gym is a form of sexual harassment to men because if a man comes on to her she could file sexual harassment charges against him. What is he supposed to do, pluck his eyes out of their sockets? We cannot control what others wear but you as a woman of God should be mindful of what you wear because the last thing you want is a man that is looking to fulfill his lust.

You are probably asking, "What makes this man think he can talk to me this way?" Is it because I am an author? No. Is it because of my success? No. Success doesn't qualify anyone to speak with authority in the Kingdom of God. I only need to give you two of my qualifications. First, I am a man; all man and will never be anything less than a man, who at one

Why Do the Bad Ones Keep Coming to You?

time didn't know the Lord and lived as an agent of lust. Now I live as the faithful husband of **one wife**. Secondly, I am a father of four daughters who are 13, 11, 9 and 1. As a father it is my desire for all of them to be happily married to good, God-fearing, Holy-Ghost-filled men. I have one son that I train in manhood (he will be a good man). I am not just a natural father but God has anointed me to be a Spiritual Father. You are my daughters and I must instruct, guide and warn you of these subtle earthly and spiritual dangers in relationships.

> *For even if you had ten thousand others to teach you about Christ, you have only one spiritual father. For I became your father in Christ Jesus when I preached the Good News to you.*
>
> *1 Corinthians 4:15 (New Living Translation)*

Nine Types of People to Avoid in Church

Fornicators

Liars

Non-Believers

Non-Spiritual

Compromisers

Non-Bible Readers

Non-Praying

Nosey

Busybodies

The Body Speaks

After processing a woman's body language men usually come to a conclusion: you are giving signals that say you are open game for quick and easy sex, or they will look at your body language and say, "She's a

Why Do the Bad Ones Keep Coming to You?

good girl who's handling her business and she doesn't play. If I want to get with her I need to come correct or don't come to her at all".

I'm not saying you should dress like Aunt Jemima or like you are stuck in a time warp, but I will say you should be prudent in selecting the clothing you wear. It will be hard for you to dress like models, TV stars and secular singers and not give off the wrong signal. Be mindful of what your body language is saying.

When Eve came near the forbidden tree Satan must have noticed she would not even touch the tree, which showed she had an attitude and was up set about something concerning that tree. It is important for you to know Satan is not a mind reader. Only God knows the inward thoughts. Only God is omniscient. The devil has an eye for reading body language and so do a lot of men. The next thing that gave Eve away were the words she spoke concerning the command God gave Adam (her husband) about the tree. Eve said, *"God says we must not eat it or even touch it, or we will die"* (Genesis 3:3*)*.

Did you read that verse in Genesis 3:3? It contains something in it that should not be there. Read it again. What did you notice?

Satan sensed the woman had a chip on her shoulder so he moved in the most cunning way he could without chasing her off. He finds the choicest of words to test if what he was reading from her body language was really what he was seeing. He could have come right out with what he really wanted to say, which was, "God doesn't care about you because He's hiding something from you and He is a liar". Satan didn't do that until the time was right. First he wanted to see how Eve would respond to his statement put in the form of a question.

"Really?" Satan said "Did God say you must not eat any of the fruit in the garden?" (Genesis 3:1). The question is phrased in a way that it corners you into a response, any response. The response will let the devil know where you are. He really needed a comeback from Eve, for her to say something, anything.

Why Do the Bad Ones Keep Coming to You?

What would be Eve's reply? If she is happy with where she is then the serpent will go his way and try again some other day. If she replies with the Word of God and stands her ground on the Word the devil knows he has to flee.

> *So humble yourselves before God. Resist the devil, and he will flee from you.*
>
> James 4:7 (New Living Translation)

When the devil tempted Jesus in the wilderness he wanted Him to say **something**, but Jesus simply replied with what God said, nothing more and nothing less. He stood on the truth of the Word and Satan was not able to move Him half an inch.

If Eve is not happy or she has a chip on shoulder, and Satan has read her body language correctly then she will say something to prove the serpent's theory. Satan is ready to discredit the Word of God but he needs someone to agree with him in the earth realm, thus he wanted Eve's opinion on this forbidden tree situation.

Eve's words proved Satan did his homework and his study of her body language was as on the mark as a Michael Jordan slam-dunk. Eve said these words:

> [2] *"Of course we may eat it," the woman told him.* [3] *"It's only the fruit from the tree at the center of the garden that we are not allowed to eat. God says we must not eat it **or even touch it** or we will die".*
>
> Genesis 3:2-3 (New Living Translation)

There you have it. Satan got the response he was looking for. In verse 3 she quoted the scripture but threw in something that proved her contempt for the law of the forbidden fruit. She said **"or even touch it".** That is not what God said.

> [17] *But of the tree of the knowledge of good and evil, **thou shalt not eat of it**: for in the day that thou eatest thereof*

165

Why Do the Bad Ones Keep Coming to You?

thou shalt surely die.

Genesis 2:17

So then the second thing men will read are your words. Have you ever said something to someone weeks, months or even years ago and they came back to you and said say "I thought you said...". Yes, people look and listen for contradictions in the words you speak.

Many women of faith have surrendered their fragrance, faith and love for God because they fell for an uncommitted sex partner who tore them up. Now they are finding it hard to get connected with Jesus again because the soul tie with that lover is too strong. They will cuss mama and daddy out and anyone else who dares to stand in the way. They will disobey the Voice of the Spirit from their leaders because somebody tore them up and made them feel good. The men they select are influenced by demons who want to ravish their bodies with forbidden sex acts such as fornication, multiple partners, sale of their private acts on the internet and so on. These men will sometimes pimp the women, forcing them to have sex with male friends or prostitute them for fast cash all in the name of pleasing him and fulfilling his fantasy. Yet the man never commits to the covenant of marriage and never will because all he ever wanted was to destroy the woman's fragrance. He never loved the woman he just wanted to tear her up. The phrase "tear up" has a more insightful meaning other than just sex, it also means to be torn up and wrecked spiritually. She will soon be cast aside; maybe then she will realize **you cannot give yourself to someone who doesn't belong to you in the first place**.

Why Do the Bad Ones Keep Coming to You?

Test Your Spiritual Fragrance

1. List nine reasons why odor and smell are important on earth.

   _____ _____ _____

   _____ _____ _____

   _____ _____ _____

2. What does the word "rest" mean to an unclean spirit?

3. How does the way a woman is dressed speak to a potential husband?

4. Explain how body language works.

5. How did Satan know he could approach Eve with a lie?

6. What or who are the dry places?

7. What does the author mean by "getting torn up"?

8. What does having water mean?

9. Why does the unclean spirit keep coming back?

10. If you are having a hard time getting out of a bad situation whom should you spend time with?

Chapter 15

What Do You Smell Like?

*E*lizabeth Taylor, J-Lo, Britney Spears, Mariah Carey and Beyonce' Knowles all have their own perfume labels. Although their fame and success has helped them sell expensive perfumes it cannot buy good relationships. It takes the anointing of the Apothecary (Jesus Christ) to make you smell good in the spirit. Their designer fragrances may smell good in the natural, but in the spirit they stink.

Jesus knows how to wash, cleanse and perfume you. He knows how to make you smell so good that God the Father, the All Sufficient One is joyously excited about having a relationship with you. If God is pleased by your fragrance then how much more will one of His earthly sons? You have been anointed by Jesus to have a godly relationship with a husband. You should smell of **camphire**, *love that comes with a word of wisdom;* **spikenard**, *joy that comes with a word of knowledge;* **saffron**, *peace that comes with faith;* **calamus**, *the spice that is longsuffering and comes with healing;* **cinnamon** *spice, with its gentleness and the working of miracles;* **frankincense**, *goodness and the gift of prophecy;* **myrrh**, *faith and discerning of spirits;* **aloes**, *meekness and divers tongues; and finally the* **chief spices**, *of temperance and the interpretation of tongues.*

Let's examine our list of earthly perfume makers and some of their relationships to see what fruits they have produced. Elizabeth Taylor hasn't had good fortune in any of her relationships. She's been married eight times and all have failed – eight marriages. That's more than the woman at the well (John 4:16-18). She obviously had no problem getting a man but apparently has a problem maintaining the relationship. I wonder what type of anointing is in her perfume; it can't be a good one. Yet women wear her perfume as though it has an anointing that will attract a

What Do You Smell Like?

strong and lasting relationship. Jennifer Lopez, a.k.a. J-Lo has become a well-known celebrity with a popular fragrance. She has been engaged several times and married three times, all with big fanfare but I wonder what type of anointing is in her perfume, it can't be good. Yet her fragrances are flying off the shelves. Britney Spears, Mariah Carey and Beyonce' Knowles are all attractive women but good looks do not guarantee healthy relationships and blessed marriages. Their names are on bottles of perfume but that's about it. Britney married a man who fathered children by another woman (not his wife) and she is having a hard time keeping his attention on her and on their new family. Mariah wears next to nothing in all of her public appearances and has finally landed herself another man, but they are not married. She had a failed marriage yet she is selling a product of attraction. Beyonce' is always on the "most beautiful people" list but she has had an up and down relationship with Jay Z, a rapper who calls himself "Jehovah god". They are not married and there are no known plans for a wedding. I wonder what type of blessing her fragrance brings to those who wear it.

Most of the fragrances for men are made by well-known homosexuals, yet people consistently buy and wear their products. I wonder if the spirit operating in those men comes through the fragrance that bears their name.

I'm not saying you should not wear the perfume of the women that I just mentioned. I only desire to show you the spiritual side of a perfume maker and the people who wear their fragrance and show that some perfumes may indeed smell good but the lifestyle of its maker stinks.

The apothecary is a very skilled perfume maker who must be knowledgeable about weights and measurements so the perfume gives forth the precise scent. Jesus is our highly skilled perfume maker and He has sweet spices for you to wear that will give you favor with God and man; favor in the heavens and on earth. You smell so good when you have Jesus. Your scent is highly desirable when you have spent time with Jesus; because of your intimate closeness the smell of His garments has rubbed off on you. You smell good when you keep yourself in the will of God, when the life you speak of is the life that you live. That smells good. When a good man smells the trials of your life with God on your side he is

What Do You Smell Like?

pleased because your scent is delightful when you put on Christ.

I would rather put on Jesus than anyone else because He is the one who has favor with God and man (Luke 2:52). If you wear what He wore then you will be vested with favor. When you are anointed with Jesus' fragrance you have the high privilege of standing by His side as a Queen of the King of Righteousness.

> *[6]Thy throne, O God, is for ever and ever: the sceptre of thy kingdom is a right sceptre. [7] Thou lovest righteousness, and hatest wickedness: therefore God, thy God, hath anointed thee with the oil of gladness above thy fellows. [8]* **All thy garments smell of myrrh, and aloes, and cassia,** *out of the ivory palaces, whereby they have made thee glad. [9] Kings' daughters were among thy honourable women: upon thy right hand did stand the queen in gold of Ophir.*
>
> *Psalm 45:6-9 (KJV)*

Verse 8 of Psalm 45 tells us what Jesus smelled like. He wore myrrh, aloes and the sweet smell of cassia on all of His garments. When He healed the woman with the issue of blood we now know what He smelled like— myrrh aloes and sweet cassia. When Jesus spoke life to Jarius' daughter and raised her from death we now know what He smelled like; myrrh, aloes and sweet cassia. When He cast out devils and raised the dead boy in the city of Nain we have knowledge of how He smelled, like Emmanuel, "God with us" –myrrh, aloes and cassia.

Myrrh	------	Father
Aloe	------	Son
Cassia	------	Holy Ghost

These Three are One (I John 5:7).

170

What Do You Smell Like?

Rate Your Spiritual Scent

1. Do you think divorce is a good thing?

2. Do you want to be like any secular artist?

3. Do you think Beyonce' Knowles is a spiritual role model?

4. Would you like to live your life like Elizabeth Taylor?

5. Is Jennifer Lopez marriage material?

6. Do you have a homosexual male as a close friend?

7. To the best of your knowledge do you know if Mariah Carey lives her life for Jesus? (Yes or No, explain why)

8. Have you ever seen or heard any reports about Britney Spears going to church regularly?

9. Is there salvation or eternal life in any other name than the name of Jesus?

If you answered *no to all of the questions* your scent for this chapter is excellent.

If you answered *yes to one to three* of these your scent is good but can improve.

If you answered *yes to four and more* your spiritual scent is bad and you are in need of a new anointing.

Chapter 16

The Spiritual Fragrance Poem

The following is a poem the Spirit of the Lord gave me regarding the fragrance of a woman. It is very short but will have a long lasting effect. I think it will help you further understand the concept of the spiritual fragrance of a woman. I thought this poem was important enough to make it a chapter in the book. This is the perfect place to pause and reflect on what you have read so far.

She is more beautiful than the most decorated garden or tower.

Her fragrance is sweeter than a field full of the most fragrant flower.

Her life is abundant with love and grace, like a refreshing April shower.

Her ways are as colorful as a rainbow,
more attractive to the eyes than a field covered with snow.

Her fragrance is rare we know.

She is the Lord's property, because her fruits like His do show.

Her gifts are full of variety like a rainbow.

Healing, Tongues, Prophecy and Mo'

Wherever she goes she leaves a blessed spiritual scent.

Frankincense, Myrrh, Calamus and Mint.

Who can find such a woman as this?

If you follow her fragrance you will never miss.

The Spiritual Fragrance Poem

Test from the Poem

1. What did she have in abundance?

2. What made her the Lord's property?

3. What four aromas does she leave behind?

4. How can anyone find her?

5. What three gifts does the poem mention?

6. What are two signs of weather mentioned in the poem?

7. What sign of weather is mentioned twice?

Chapter 17

Dead Flies

"Dead flies cause the ointment of the apothecary to send forth a stinking savour: so doth a little folly him that is in reputation for wisdom and honour."

Ecclesiastes 10:1 (KJV)

Dead flies can smell like a large road kill in the summer heat. It's amazing something so small can have such a strong and terrible smell. One fly won't produce much of a scent but hundreds of dead flies in a concentrated area can send forth a foul odor. Just like flies can stink up something meant for good so can foolish living and unclean behavior ruin a person meant to live a life of wisdom and honor. One foolish mistake can spoil your perfume.

Allow me a little space to talk about the fly and its importance in the verse above. **Beel** is a Hebrew word meaning "lord" or "lord of". **Beel** is best known when it is associated with the name **Zebub** (flies), thus **Beelzebub** is the lord of the flies. Satan is the leader of swarms of flies. Whenever flies enter a room they distract people. That is what Beelzebub does, distract God's people so they lose track of their destiny.

[1] *And the fifth angel sounded, and I saw a **star** (Satan) fall from heaven unto the earth: and to him was given the key of the bottomless pit.* [2] *And he opened the bottomless pit; and there arose a smoke out of the pit, as the smoke of a great furnace; and the sun and the air were darkened by reason of the smoke of the pit.* [3] *And there came out of the smoke locusts upon the earth: and unto them was given power, as the scorpions of the earth have power.* [4] *And it*

174

Dead Flies

was commanded them that they should not hurt the grass of the earth, neither any green thing, neither any tree; but only those men which have not the seal of God in their foreheads.

Revelation 9:1-4 (KJV)

[11] *And they had **a king over them**, which is the angel of the bottomless pit, whose name in the Hebrew tongue is Abaddon, but in the Greek tongue hath his name Apollyon.*

Revelation 9:11 (KJV)

How many times have you been distracted by the man fly, the job fly, the family fly or the mental fly? The devil sends flies to leave you confused, speechless and far off course from God's plan.

How many sisters do you see being distracted by man flies? They were at one time focused, growing, faithful, loving and praising God. The Lord was blessing them. They were growing in the Word, making it to all the prayer meetings and then it happened—distracted by a fly. I've seen many sisters hold on and trust God for years and just as the Spirit of the Lord begins to release a Word of Knowledge on what God is planning for them, the flies come. Soon they are out of the church and living in sin. I noticed certain patterns of behaviors in the sisters who become distracted by flies.

- Continue attending church but rush out as soon as service is over.
- Dress better and start wearing a little more make up.
- Still praise God, but not with the same intensity.
- Moody in church, attitude starts to stink.
- Stop volunteering at the church, making excuses as to why.
- Continue going to Sunday service, but not to prayer or Bible study.
- Miss important events in the church when they never would before.
- Purposely distance themselves from others in the church.
- Stop coming to church.

Dead Flies

All of these attitudes grow worse and worse if the fly can make a landing (you know what I mean). That fly will cause your spiritual fragrance of joy, faithfulness, peace and focus to stink. If your man won't go to church and he's keeping you out, he's a fly. If you are following a fly you are behaving foolishly. Wake up. Shake him off and come to yourself. One fly in your perfume will have a negative effect on your glorious aroma from Jesus, and a defected aroma attracts more flies. The one curious fly that landed in your fragrance will leave behind the stench of death. Good men don't want a woman surrounded by flies; flies calling your cel phone, flies giving you hugs and asking how have you been. Good men will ask, "How do these flies know you so well?" and then move on because you apparently have a history with flies. Men know what other men are all about. A man knows if flies surround the woman he's interested in then chances are her ointment contains a few flies as well. Flies will come at you in different shapes and forms with all types of sexual appetites and addictions. However, what **you do** will determine whether they get in or stay out. If you are in the right place with God the flies cannot come nigh your dwelling.

Could the answer be laid open in the wisdom of Ecclesiastes 10:1? Could there be something in this verse that speaks to your relational dilemma? Let's break it down. The verse begins with two words: **dead flies**. Dead describes the object in the ointment, in this case the Preacher Solomon uses flies. Flies in the perfume are bad enough but the verse says they are dead, lifeless and foul smelling.

Flies are a symbol of something that defiles or makes unclean. Whether dead or alive, a fly will make people throw away something they enjoy like an ice cream cone, a sandwich or a meal. They are ugly creepy little intruders that remind people of something stinky, decaying or just flat out filthy. Flies annoy people by landing on their legs, arms and faces over and over again until the person can't take it anymore and puts everything on hold trying to kill it.

Egypt was destroyed by ten plagues and one of them was flies. Notice the following verses.

Dead Flies

*[20] Next the LORD told Moses, "Get up early in the morning and meet Pharaoh as he goes down to the river. Say to him, 'this is what the LORD says: Let my people go, so they can worship me. [21] If you refuse, I will send **swarms of flies** throughout Egypt. Your homes will be filled with them, and the ground will be covered with them. [22] But it will be very different in the land of Goshen, where the Israelites live. No flies will be found there. Then you will know that I am the LORD and that I have power even in the heart of your land. [23] I will make a clear distinction between your people and my people. This miraculous sign will happen tomorrow.' " [24] And the LORD did just as he had said. There were **terrible swarms of flies** in Pharaoh's palace and in every home in Egypt. **The whole country was thrown into chaos by the flies.***

Exodus 8:20-24 (New Living Translation)

Notice the Bible says swarms of flies, meaning there were many different types and mixtures that invaded Egypt. One particular fly in Africa was known to be poisonous; called the dog fly (stable fly), a bloodsucker that primarily attacked animals, but in the absence of an animal host would also bite men. Of the 21,000 known species of flies, each one has a different way of eating. Some suck, bite and vomit on their food; others use their needle-shaped mouths to pierce the skin. Some species feast at sores and open wounds while others are attracted to moist places like the eyes, nose and mouth. They also differ in body shapes, some big, medium and small; some can grow to be the size of a human hand while others are so small you can barely see or feel them.

"No flies will be found there" (Genesis 8:22)

Don't you think God's people were glad to be without flies in Goshen? If you are in the place where God wants you to be and doing what pleases Him then you too will be fly free. It is when we become rebellious, self-directed, and unyielding to the voice of the Lord that the flies come. You must work at being fly free.

Dead Flies

I remember reading about Abraham when he cut animals in half to make a covenant with God. He prepared the animals as God commanded but then buzzards gathered around the Holy sacrifice. Abraham would not have it. That old man chased those birds away because if they defiled his sacrifice his future blessings from God could have been ruined (Genesis 15:10-11). That is the same attitude you must have when it comes to flies gathering around, seeking to damage your beautiful aroma. They are not concerned about your sacrifice, your chastity or your future because they cannot appreciate the value. To them, virginity is a joke and holy living is a fairytale; they see nothing wrong with having sex outside of marriage. They place high value on getting into something that is not theirs to begin with. Your body does not belong to a man if he is not your husband, therefore he cannot place a demand on it (I Corinthians 7:4).

Didn't your parents tell you time and time again how dirty it was to spray perfume on an unwashed behind? People who put on perfume without bathing first ruin the aroma of that fragrance and defeat the entire purpose for wearing it. Fragrance will not cover up a dirty body's smell; it will only magnify and highlight the stink. It doesn't matter how beautiful and concentrated the fragrance is, the stench of body odor will overpower the sweet aroma of the perfume. The funk will win. That is what sin and foolishness does, it ruins the spiritual perfume.

Why do women who claim to be serving God expect the Lord to send them a husband when they are unfaithful in their commitment to Him? That is just like spraying perfume onto someone who has not showered in days. That doesn't make sense does it? You are supposed to bathe first then add the fragrance. You must allow the Word of God to clean you up before receiving the anointing of a spiritual aroma. I am telling you Jesus will not invest His precious anointing on someone who cannot stay clean and refuses to wash daily in the Word of God. So many in the church hit and miss; they are up and down, in and out, saved and unsaved. It is time to decide what you want to be. Do you want to be a wife or do you want to be used as a second choice? Do you want the will of God for your life or do you want your own way? Choose ye this day whom ye will serve; will it be God or man (Joshua 24:15)?

Dead Flies

Fan the flies away from your blessed fragrance; they will damage the work of God in your life. Once they get into your house they will land in your fragrance and lay eggs known as larva. Flies exist to multiply and take over until your fragrance is no longer the fragrance of the LORD but the defilement of the flies.

Why do good women of God continue to attract men of bad character? They may be men physically but they are boys when it comes to commitments, responsibilities, making decisions and setting goals; who like to be known as pimps, players, ballers, dogs, ol' dirty's, hustlers, dealers, thugs, gangsters, slangers, etc. If you put all of those titles, names or whatever you want to call them together what do you get? A room full of flies. Men who refer to relationships with women as "The Game" are flies. You've heard some of their childish sayings: "don't hate the player hate the game", "player hater", "drama with baby mama". These statements and others like them have taken on a life of their own thanks to men who pride themselves on having more than one woman without ever committing themselves unless serving a life sentence in prison. Flies live in open and unashamed sin, it doesn't matter who is looking. Flies just want to have fly babies, ride in fly cars, live in fly apartments, have fly incomes, have fly friends and wear fly clothes.

As a spiritual father I've counseled countless men and women, husbands and wives, and even children. I found most men who refer to themselves as one of the slang names above, do so because they were either hurt by women (including mothers, grand mothers, aunts, etc), have come to distrust women, or don't know how to treat them.

I remember a situation where I had to deal with a demonic fly. I used to work as a case manager in a mental institution. I was known by all of my co-workers as a man of prayer so they came to me with all kinds of personal problems, knowing if I prayed God would hear me and move on their behalf, which He did repeatedly. One day one of my co-workers came into my office crying and very upset. She asked if I would pray for her friend who had been seeing this guy for about a month and ever since then she started acting crazy; pulling her clothes off, getting on all fours barking like a dog, running down the street half naked screaming as if

179

Dead Flies

someone is chasing her, going into long trances and not going to work. I asked had they been having sex. She said yes. I asked "What does this guy do for a living; does he work? Is he a drug dealer or a drug user?" She said he was on crack. I asked if her friend was using drugs with him. She said no, she had never done drugs and would have told her if she did. Her friend showed up on the job and I was called to the parking lot to meet her. I grabbed her hands and rebuked the devil and cast the unclean spirits out of her. Once I knew she was free I told her she could not have sex with that man or any other man who was not her husband. I told her those demonic spirits entered her through intercourse and that drug spirits, sorcery and spirits of lust were transferred to her through sexual contact. Flies died in her perfume and caused it to give out a stinking smell. She became one with him through sex which caused her to act like a person who was on drugs, but thanks be to God for the prayers of the righteous.

> *[15] Should a man take his body, which belongs to Christ, and join it to a prostitute? Never! [16] And don't you know that if a man joins himself to a prostitute, he becomes one body with her?*

> *1 Corinthians 6:15-16 (New Living Translation)*

Fornication is the only sin listed in the Bible as being done against the body because of soul ties and idol worship. As a believer in Christ your body is the temple where God lives, but when you fornicate you remove God from His temple and put the man you are having sex with in His place. As Paul says, if you commit fornication you are offending your body to the one you are having sex with.

Dead Flies

Identify Your Flies

Circle the ones that have flown into your life.
Use the blank lines to add any that aren't already listed.

Fornication	Frustration	Confusion	Worry
Jealousy	Shamefulness	Masturbation	Adultery
Gossip	Headaches	Fear	Lying
Tiredness	Sexual fantasies	Confrontations	Gloominess
Self-centeredness	Bickering	Unforgiveness	Alcohol
Drugs	Insomnia	Sleepiness	Depression
Hatred	Overly possessive	Loneliness	Stubbornness
Shyness	Insecurity	Judging	Temper
Envy	Hopelessness	Discouragement	Anger
Bitterness	Spite	Laziness	Nervousness
Sensitivity	Trust issues	Over eating	Grief
Sadness	Weakness	Compromise	Not eating
Pity	Rape	Stress	Addictions
Poverty	Lack of Focus	No Joy	Disorder
Dysfunctional	Despised		

_____   _____   _____   _____

_____   _____   _____   _____

It is important to know you are not claiming these but instead exposing and bringing to light the ungodly mindsets and behaviors by identifying them. Jesus said the healthy do not need a doctor but those who have identified their sicknesses are the ones that will get the help.

Dead Flies

¹⁵ And it came to pass, that, as Jesus sat at meat in his house, many publicans and sinners sat also together with Jesus and his disciples: for there were many, and they followed him. ¹⁶ And when the scribes and Pharisees saw him eat with publicans and sinners, they said unto his disciples, How is it that he eateth and drinketh with publicans and sinners? ¹⁷ **When Jesus heard it, he saith unto them, They that are whole have no need of the physician, but they that are sick: I came not to call the righteous, but sinners to repentance.**

Mark 2:15-17 (KJV)

Breaking Soul Ties with Flies

Dead flies will not remove themselves. They must be eliminated by force by the perfume wearer or by someone who has the authority and power to remove them.

And they were all amazed, and spake among themselves, saying, What a word is this! for with authority and power he commandeth the unclean spirits, and they come out.

Luke 4:36 (KJV)

Why would anyone allow flies to remain in their anointment? Maybe they have developed a familiar connection with the fly and are desensitized to the foul odor and behavior. Some people never achieve full deliverance because they like a particular behavior and have a kinship and friendship with the unclean spirit; they refuse to abandon the relationship. If you are in the midst of a filthy and foul odor you will eventually become desensitized to the stench and walk around in it as though all is well. Someone else could walk in from the fresh clean air and as soon as the door opens they can smell the foul spirit of the house. That is precisely what God's ministers do, they enter into the room of someone's spirit and smell the foul odor of the enemy even when the person who is in bondage cannot.

Dead Flies

Fly Removal Exercise

List Nine Possible Flies In Your Ointment

1. _____
2. _____
3. _____
4. _____
5. _____
6. _____
7. _____
8. _____
9. _____

Now take every name/item on your list, and one by one say: "Lord Jesus I receive freedom and deliverance from this spirit". Begin to denounce them forcibly; one by one and name by name, breathing deeply (you may get choked up or feel like vomiting with a watery or a foamy mouth). Do not stop until you know it is gone and then move on to the next one. Continue to let the flies know they are not wanted and you want them out of your life right now in the name of Jesus. I recommend you do this with an experienced prayer warrior.

Dead Flies

PRAYER

Father, in the Name of Jesus, I confess there are flies in my life. I also confess your blood was shed for the cleansing of my sins.

I ask that you deliver me from every ungodly soul-tie I have. I declare I am free from all forms of bondage and any residue of the flies I just confessed. I am also free from any associated spirits of those flies.

I declare I am totally free because your word says he whom the Son has set free is totally free. Jesus I ask you to replace and fill every empty place from which the flies have fallen and fill me completely with your Presence, Power and Spirit.

I thank you that I am fly free now. Amen

Chapter 18

Put a Lid on It

You are a private garden, my treasure, my bride! You are like a spring that no one else can drink from, a fountain of my own.

Song of Solomon 4:12 (New Living Translation)

How do flies get into a bottle of perfume? "Dead flies cause the ointment of the apothecary to send forth a stinking savour: so doth a little folly him that is in reputation for wisdom and honour." (Ecclesiastes 10:1) Are flies attracted to the smell of perfume? What are they doing around something that smells good? Flies enter a perfume simply because the lid was left off. They are curious little pests that will land on anything exposed. If the lid is left off the perfume and a fly goes inside and dies is it the fly's fault? No, it is up to the fragrance owner to protect their anointed oil. Flies are not attracted to the beautiful scent of perfume; the enjoyment is in finding something with a foul smell but they will try something new. The perfume jar of your body (which holds the sweet fragrance) should remain sealed until your husband removes the lid.

Desire to be what Solomon said about his new wife; a private garden, meaning not open to the public. Private means there are restrictions on who gets in and when. This is a lovely Biblical picture of a woman in control of her spirit, her emotions and her body. Although there may be times when your emotions and hormones are begging you to give in to the desires of your flesh, don't do it. Let the reward of being a private garden of the Lord and your future husband serve as the motivation to take control of your body. Even if someone has entered in the past, lock your garden and keep it private until the right time, i.e. your wedding night.

185

Put a Lid on It

Take a moment to seriously think about this. Suppose you planted a garden in your back yard with a tall fence around it to protect all of your favorite herbs, fruits and vegetables; you watered daily, painstakingly pruned before they even sprouted leaves, and waited all summer long for them to ripen. The garden was so precious you put a plastic owl in the middle to keep the birds away and personally plucked the bugs off the leaves, dreaming of the day when you could enjoy the harvest. Who did you plant those foods for? Would you allow strangers to walk into your garden and take whatever they wanted?

This is what happens to women who have an open lid policy on sexual relations with men they've never married. They are letting strangers spoil their garden. You must be careful to keep the lid on your anointing because once you meet your husband he may hear about the strangers that trampled through your garden spoiling his fruit. Whether you realize it or not you are the property of your husband. Even though you have not met him yet your body still belongs to him, for his enjoyment only.

The apostle Paul told the men when they have pre-marital sex with a single female woman they are defrauding their brother by opening up his gift (I Thessalonians 4:3-6). They have essentially opened someone else's package and stolen the precious fruits reserved for the woman's future husband.

The Bible says he that finds a wife finds a good thing (Proverbs 18:22). This verse does not mean he finds someone else's wife but rather finds a single woman who is seriously committed to maintaining her garden in private, which is a good thing. The private garden also shows her loyalty and commitment to her fiancé. On the spiritual side you are the private property of the Lord Jesus who purchased you with His own blood.

> *"In whom ye also trusted, after that ye heard the word of truth, the gospel of your salvation: in whom also after that ye believed, **ye were sealed** with that holy Spirit of promise, Which is the earnest of our inheritance, until the redemption of the purchased possession, unto the praise of his glory."*

Put a Lid on It

Ephesians 1:13-14 (KJV)

The Bible says you were sealed with the Holy Spirit of promise. You are covered by the Holy Spirit, which seals you from the pollutions in the world. You can break this seal whenever you want, but it is to your advantage to keep it intact. This seal ensures your fragrance will remain pure so you can please the heart of God, spread the Gospel of Jesus Christ and draw your husband into your life. Complications begin to unfold when people break the seal outside of God's will; things like unwanted children, abortions, sexually transmitted diseases, unholy soul ties, fading faith, confusion, more bad decisions, etc.

When God began to reveal the blessings of the covenant He changed Abram's name to Abraham (father of a multitude). He then told Abraham to surrender his loins by circumcision. Abraham and every single male in his household had to cut their private area as a sign of connection to the Lord (Genesis 17:5-13). People charge down to the altar vowing to give their heart to Jesus but don't surrender their loins (private parts). They leave that same altar of commitment and return to their shack-up partner or exchange numbers with someone later on and have an unholy hookup. Some come to church to receive Jesus as Lord, but only over certain problems and not their entire lives. This is reminiscent of so many women because they get lonely, fed up, weary of waiting for God to send a man so they leave the lid off and let a fly hang around until he gets a chance to land in their perfume. When asked why he is hanging around so much, the woman usually replies "We're just friends". When the fly falls in he does not bring life or add to the blessed aroma; he leaves the stench of death.

Fornication is a sin. Living in fornication will hinder your walk with Christ and prevent you from entering heaven (I Corinthians 6:9-10 and Hebrews 13:4). The Bible tells us the wages of sin is death (Romans 6:23). If there are flies in your ointment it is only because **you** took the lid off. Maybe you are letting a fly hang around 'just because' or 'just in case' God doesn't send a husband. Maybe you are trying to convert the fly and bring him to the Lord to get saved, not realizing **you cannot convert a fly** through your own efforts. It would take a miracle of God, of which you cannot perform. Soon you will figure out flies and perfume don't mix;

Put a Lid on It

there is no harmony between the two. So now your jar of wonderful smelling perfume has become a stinking cesspool, good for nothing but attracting more flies.

Every man of God would love to have the thrill, the satisfaction and the joy of experiencing what Solomon says of his new bride. He said she was a private garden fenced in, with fruits and vegetables that none other had ever tasted. She was his treasure; the one he found and had the pleasure of opening for himself. He went on to say she was a spring of water that no one else could drink from; a fountain dedicated solely to him.

If the man of God can smell dead flies in your fragrance he may not stick around and get to know you better unless he is a risk taker. What do I mean by dead flies? Dead flies are the spirits of men with whom you have had sexual experiences. The relationship may have ended long ago but you still have soul ties to them. The soul tie links the two of you together as one. Sometimes soul ties bring on feelings that are not yours, thoughts that belong to him, confusion, curses, poverty, and even sexual lust for other females because of a soul tie through sexual contact.

Sex is more than just the act of sex; it is intercourse. It is to become one in spirit with that person; to tie your destiny with theirs. ***Inter*** is a prefix occurring in Latin loan words, meaning "between", "among", "in the midst of", "mutually", "reciprocally", "together", "during." *Inter* is used all the time to bring two things, places, times, sentences and people together into one: Intercom, Internet, Interchange, Interlock, International, Interlude, Intercept, Intercede, Intermarriage, Interference, Interface, Intercross, Intergrowth, etc. If you looked in the dictionary the one thing they all have in common is the prefix *inter* makes their definitions bring the two objects together.

Dead flies are painful scars from failed relationships, divorces or loss of a loved one. Dead flies can be a lack of trust and respect for men because you feel all men are dogs, simply because dogs are all you've had. Dead flies are unclean spirits left unexposed and unresolved for you. Dead flies can also represent baggage from the past that you carry around in your perfume as you go from place to place and from man to man. Dead flies

Put a Lid on It

could also be a spirit of **anger** and **bitterness** that rises up whenever you think about how someone mistreated you, let you down, hurt and used you; or when you hear about another woman finding a good man especially if you know she didn't have it all together, yet you are still left alone. These are dead flies and they will make your fragrance stink.

Here are seven things that will remove the dead flies:

1. Resist evil thinking (I Corinthians 15:33).
2. Think on good, pure, holy and happy things (Philippians 4:8-9).
3. Resist evil speaking (Psalm 34:13).
4. Talk about things you know will be pleasing to God (Psalm 34:1).
5. Resist evil company (Psalm 1:1)
6. Communicate with good godly people (Hebrews 10:23-25).
7. Resist condemning yourself for the mistakes you've made in the past (Philippians 3:13-14).

Chapter 19

Mary's Alabaster Box

*M*uch speculation surrounds Mary Magdalene and the things she may have been involved in before she became a follower of Jesus. This viewpoint was magnified thanks to the success of the *Da Vinci Code*, which depicted her as secretly marrying Jesus and bearing His children. Even though the Bible does not share all the details of her life, that story is absolutely ridiculous. She was mainly known in the Bible for two things; first she came from a town named Magdala thus the name Mary Magdalene, and secondly Jesus cast seven demons out of her (Mark 16:9).

One day Mary came into a room full of people and anointed the feet of Jesus (John 12:1-3). She anointed Jesus with her fragrance because He had set her completely free. The very expensive ointment was called spikenard and came in an alabaster box. Spikenard was too expensive to just store in anything; in those days it was worth about one full year's salary. Alabaster is a translucent stone considered by the ancients to be the best way to preserve precious ointments. It had no handles, but a long neck that had to be broken off in order to pour out the fragrance inside (Mark 14:3 and Matthew 26:7).

Once the fragrance was poured inside, the alabaster box was sealed. The only way to get to the fragrance was to break the box, thereby reinforcing the high importance of the contents. Since spikenard was so expensive people did not open it except for very, very special occasions. I saw on the news recently that someone paid $10 million for a bottle of wine. Now you know when they open that bottle it will be a very grand occasion!

As you can see Mary made a tremendous personal sacrifice to anoint Jesus. The alabaster box and its contents was something she held in very

Mary's Alabaster Box

high regard because she brought it to Jesus, the man who set her free from her past. Seven not only indicates the amount of unclean spirits cast out of her but as the number of completion, seven points more to her being completely bound by those devils; once she was freed she knew it was all because of Jesus.

> *And being in Bethany in the house of Simon the leper, as he sat at meat, there came a woman having an alabaster box of ointment of spikenard very precious; and she brake the box, and poured it on his head.*
>
> *Mark 14:3 (KJV)*

Mary broke her seal for Jesus. Who have you broken your seal for? How special was the occasion? Was it your wedding night? It is only when we break ourselves from our own will and desires of the flesh that the fragrance fills our lives.

> *Then took Mary a pound of ointment of spikenard, very costly, and anointed the feet of Jesus, and wiped his feet with her hair: and **the house was filled with the odour of the ointment.***
>
> *John 12:3 (KJV)*

Your Alabaster Box

You must invest in your alabaster box; it is your body. Your body is the vessel that carries the precious fragrance inside. It is the temple of God for the Holy Ghost to dwell inside of you (I Corinthians 3:16).

Take care of your alabaster box; no one else can do it better than you. Keep it well preserved and beautifully maintained. If you are anxious about your personal appearance it will affect the way you present yourself to others. Being overweight or otherwise unhealthy can affect the way you feel about yourself and how you think others perceive you. Lack of exercise and personal fitness, poor eating habits, smoking cigarettes and alcohol and drug abuse all seriously affect your health, resulting in numerous illnesses such as high blood pressure, diabetes, heart disease,

Mary's Alabaster Box

kidney failure, lung disease and certain types of cancer, just to name a few. You've heard it time and again that getting a healthy body begins with a nutritious diet and regular exercise. This is not meant to start a lecture on the importance of getting in shape. The focus should be on making lifestyle changes to improve your overall health and then being diligent to maintain it. Don't feel pressured to torture yourself into becoming the Hollywood ideal of what a beautiful woman should be. God made all of us different individuals for a reason; everyone was not meant to be the same size and shape. Take pride in your unique characteristics, appearance, and style. Know there is no other woman in the world quite like you and God has someone searching for a wife with your exact qualities.

You are fearfully and wonderfully made (Psalm 139:14), and with the precious gift of your alabaster box comes the responsibility to maintain its beauty and value. You know what areas of your personal health needs improvement, but talk with your doctor before starting any diet or exercise plan. You should also get annual check ups; there is absolutely nothing wrong with your faith just because you go to the doctor. Take pride in keeping a polished appearance; clothing, hair, skin and nails. It doesn't have to be expensive either, just so you are neat, clean and attractive through self-confidence, not pricey products. Take the time to pamper yourself. You don't need to spend a lot of money. It may be a manicure or pedicure, taking a trip to the spa or whatever you enjoy that leaves you feeling beautiful inside and out. When you *feel* beautiful it shows.

Your Spikenard

Your spikenard is inside your alabaster box. The Bible says your body is the temple of the Holy Ghost to dwell in (I Corinthians 3:16) and Jesus said He would put His Spirit in you (John 14:17) and on you (Joel 2:28). This represents the indwelling of the Holy Ghost. He is the spice given unto you and He needs proper upkeep and encouragement through your clean and obedient lifestyle. You can do spiritual exercises to strengthen the presence and power of the Holy Ghost in you. The exercise is to live a life that is pleasing to God by avoiding the entrapments and entanglements of the world, the flesh, and Satan.

Mary's Alabaster Box

[16] This I say then, Walk in the Spirit, and ye shall not fulfil the lust of the flesh. [17] For the flesh lusteth against the Spirit, and the Spirit against the flesh: and these are contrary the one to the other: so that ye cannot do the things that ye would. [18] But if ye be led of the Spirit, ye are not under the law. [19] Now the works of the flesh are manifest, which are these; Adultery, fornication, uncleanness, lasciviousness, [20] Idolatry, witchcraft, hatred, variance, emulations, wrath, strife, seditions, heresies, [21] Envyings, murders, drunkenness, revellings, and such like: of the which I tell you before, as I have also told you in time past, that they which do such things shall not inherit the kingdom of God.

Galatians 5:16-21 (KJV)

Works of the flesh displease God. Here are a few things that please Him.

[1] Who may worship in your sanctuary, LORD? Who may enter your presence on your holy hill?

*[2] Those who **lead blameless lives** and **do what is right**, **speaking the truth from sincere hearts**.*

*[3] Those **who refuse to slander others or harm their neighbors or speak evil of their friends**.*

*[4] Those who **despise persistent sinners**, and **honor the faithful followers of the LORD** and **keep their promises even when it hurts**.*

*[5] Those who **do not charge interest on the money they lend,** and who **refuse to accept bribes to testify against the innocent. Such people will stand firm forever.***

Psalm 15 (New Living Translation)

Chapter 20

A Fresh Aroma

Thou anointest my head with oil…

Psalm 23:5 (KJV)

*But my horn shalt thou exalt like the horn of an unicorn: I shall be anointed with **fresh oil**.*

Psalm 92:10 (KJV)

*H*ave you made mistakes? Have you fallen from grace? Have you left your first love? It's not too late to get back up. Most of these things happen because we tried to make it on the first anointing. The anointing is an enablement; an endowment from God that gives you the power to do His will. If you run out of perfume (anointing oil) then you lose the ability to do his will. This is when you begin to compromise and lose focus. Most Christians don't have a clue about the daily anointing. The daily anointing is similar to our daily tasks; we shower, brush our teeth, get dressed and put on perfume. We should do the same in the spirit; wash in the word (Ephesians 5:26), speak the word from our mouth (Joshua 1:8), put on righteous garments (Zechariah 3:4-5) and allow Jesus' oil to cover us from top to bottom (Psalm 133:2).

David said God **anointest** (Psalm 23:5). Notice the -est at the end of the word. It speaks of continual renewing and more than one anointing. If David had said "Thou anoint" or "Thou anointed" it would refer to a limited or one-time event, but anointest is saying every day you anoint my head with new, clean, fresh and fragrant aromatic oil. The five foolish virgins were ignorant of the daily anointing and missed the Perfumer, Jesus the Bridegroom.

194

A Fresh Aroma

"The Kingdom of Heaven can be illustrated by the story of ten bridesmaids who took their lamps and went to meet the bridegroom. ² Five of them were foolish, and five were wise. ³ The five who were foolish took no oil for their lamps, ⁴ but the other five were wise enough to take along extra oil. ⁵ When the bridegroom was delayed, they all lay down and slept. ⁶ at midnight they were roused by the shout, 'Look, the bridegroom is coming! Come out and welcome him!' ⁷ "All the bridesmaids got up and prepared their lamps. ⁸ Then the five foolish ones asked the others, 'Please give us some of your oil because our lamps are going out.' ⁹ But the others replied, 'We don't have enough for all of us. Go to a shop and buy some for yourselves.' ¹⁰ "But while they were gone to buy oil, the bridegroom came, and those who were ready went in with him to the marriage feast, and the door was locked. ¹¹ Later, when the other five bridesmaids returned, they stood outside, calling, 'Sir, open the door for us!' ¹² but he called back, 'I don't know you!' ¹³ "So stay awake and be prepared, because you do not know the day or hour of my return".

Matthew 25:1-13 (New Living Translation)

The main ingredient in perfume and cologne is oil. Oil has the ability to bring all the spices together, and its bonding power causes the beautiful scent of each one to emit their fragrances in unity. Without the oil of the Holy Spirit in your life the nine fragrances will not give forth their true essence; neither will they be as sweet in the nostrils of God or man. The more oil from the Spirit you have, the more your aroma radiates its beautiful scent as God intended.

Fresh Oil – Psalm 92

In Psalm 92:10 David expressed trust and hope in the Lord by speaking as though his victory had already come to pass. He said God would exalt or raise him like the horn of a unicorn. Why did he say horn? Animal horns were a symbol of strength during Bible times. David trusted God would

A Fresh Aroma

make him stronger than his enemies. The words fresh and oil were also both used as expressions of renewal, repair, revival, and restoration, to be made anew or lifted up again. In this particular verse the word fresh means to flourish, like a luxuriant spreading tree and the word oil is referring to fatness and being fruitful. David knew God would surely cover him with a flourishing fruitfulness, all while exalting him above his enemies.

The Devil Was Anointed

> *Thou art the anointed cherub that covereth; and I have set thee so: thou wast upon the holy mountain of God; thou hast walked up and down in the midst of the stones of fire.*

> *Ezekiel 28:14 (KJV)*

As you can see the devil was anointed by God to fulfill his task in heaven as a worshipper. It is important to note Lucifer (the bright star) is now Satan (the adversary and destroyer). He still has the same anointing and abilities given him as he covered the throne of God, but now he uses it against the work and people of God. He cannot go before the Anointed One to receive a new and fresh anointing, he lost that privilege once he turned from God. The devil is forced to operate with the same anointing he was given at the beginning of time. He uses the same tricks, tactics and deceptions because he doesn't have access to use anything new.

We have the privilege of going before Jesus the Anointed Perfumer to get a new and fresh fragrance. It is not just a one-time anointing, but every day we can come before Him. Fresh oil and fresh perfume causes your heart to rejoice because that new oil represents welcoming and approval from the Lord. You have the right to go before the Lord daily and ask for more oil (His Spirit). Don't allow your anointing to become dull, tiresome and uninviting; instead receive a fresh anointing to reinvigorate your fragrance.

Chapter 21

Before You Can Lie With Your King, You Must Be Anointed

[7] *This man had a beautiful and lovely young cousin, Hadassah, who was also called Esther. When her father and mother had died, Mordecai adopted her into his family and raised her as his own daughter.* [8] *As a result of the king's decree, Esther, along with many other young women, was brought to the king's harem at the fortress of Susa and placed in Hegai's care.* [9] *Hegai was very impressed with Esther and treated her kindly. He quickly ordered a special menu for her and provided her with beauty treatments. He also assigned her seven maids specially chosen from the king's palace, and he moved her and her maids into the best place in the harem.* [10] *Esther had not told anyone of her nationality and family background, for Mordecai had told her not to.* [11] *Every day Mordecai would take a walk near the courtyard of the harem to ask about Esther and to find out what was happening to her.* [12] *before each young woman was taken to the king's bed, she was given the prescribed twelve months of beauty treatments—six months with oil of myrrh, followed by six months with special perfumes and ointments.* [13] *When the time came for her to go in to the king, she was given her choice of whatever clothing or jewelry she wanted to enhance her beauty."*

Esther 2:7-13 (New Living Translation)

Before You Can Lie with Your King, You Must Be Anointed

$\mathcal{A}$ good wife is not developed in the bedroom because she is made far before that time ever comes. Women who are developed in the bed are pros and they have a job title for what they do (prostitute); but that does not represent who you are. You, my sister, are destined to be the wife of a King. Good sex does not equal a happy marriage; there is more to a good marriage than sheet shaking and baby making. For as much as we want to take pleasure in our spouses all day every day, we cannot spend all of our time in bed because life is beckoning us to get up and move.

Too many women believe in what I call bed magic. Bed magic is when a spouse believes if they do their thing in bed then all the shortcomings, faults and mistakes in the relationship should be overlooked. They then leave the greater load of developing and maintaining the marriage to their spouse, however that is not a task that can be completed by one person. Trusting in bed magic is a mistake many people make, thinking you can satisfy your spouse with your body only. Never taking the time to consider the importance of sharing thoughts and plans through open communication, failure to share the financial responsibilities, save and invest money, pay the bills on time, raise children in the Faith of Jesus, and basic housekeeping is not only unfair to your spouse but also serves as a recipe for major trouble. Many relationships and marriages have come to an abrupt and tragic end, regardless of superb sexual relations; at least one of the two people was not ready mentally or spiritually to commit long-term. Most people only see marriage as a physical thing and totally disregard the other important components: being sacrificial, considerate, compassionate, communicative, open and honest, forsaking others for your spouse, putting your spouse first (even before children) and being accountable for your actions.

Kings can have just about any woman they want, but as you can see from the book of Esther the king was only interested in marrying a woman prepared for his bed, his home, and his life. From a man's perspective there is nothing worse than committing to a woman whom you thought was prepared for a serious relationship but find out otherwise later on. She soon becomes a burden in his life because he became a personal

Before You Can Lie with Your King, You Must Be Anointed

trainer, a parent, a daily motivator, a banker, a cook; and Lord help the king if she is overly attached to her mother who has many of the same issues. Kings are looking for women who have taken the time and gone through the necessary process of development to be more than just a good sex partner. Kings need a life mate because there are times in his life when he must to go to war, make tough decisions, etc. It is when a king is in bed that he is most vulnerable to an attempt on his life. He needs to know he can trust his queen with his very life.

Esther Was Anointed

Let us learn a few things from our girl Esther. Esther was not only a beautiful woman according to most Bible historians, but she had a spiritual fragrance that helped to enhance those outer qualities. She had something on the inside that was beautiful, peaceful and attractive. Outer beauty and a shapely figure are two nice attributes to have when it comes to attracting a regular man, but I'm talking about attracting a king. Drawing a king takes more than the physical; you need what Esther had, an awesome spiritual fragrance and a spiritual guide. As a matter of fact Esther's spiritual fragrance was a result of submitting to Mordecai. She had something amazing going on in the spirit realm, which made her even more beautiful on the outside.

The first thing to notice about Esther is her submissive spirit to Mordecai her elder cousin, spiritual father and mentor. When he gave Esther words of direction and/or instruction she listened and obeyed. She allowed Mordecai to be the lamp for her feet and he led her right into the king's heart and favor. Mordecai is the true hero of this story because he was the protection for Esther and the rest of the Jewish exiles. Chapter ten is a prime example to prove Mordecai's case. It is the shortest chapter in the entire book of Esther yet those three small verses point to the greatness of Mordecai, who is the unseen force behind Esther's glorification. He is a prophetic picture of the Holy Spirit of God, who desires to lead us into wealthy places and speaks peace to us all.

¹ And the king Ahasuerus laid a tribute upon the land, and upon the isles of the sea. ² And all the acts of his power

Before You Can Lie with Your King, You Must Be Anointed

> *and of his might, and the declaration of the greatness of Mordecai, whereunto the king advanced him, are they not written in the book of the chronicles of the kings of Media and Persia?* [3] *For Mordecai the Jew was next unto king Ahasuerus, and great among the Jews, and accepted of the multitude of his brethren, seeking the wealth of his people, and speaking peace to all his seed.*

> *Esther 10:1-3 (KJV)*

Mordecai was a father to Esther, although she was actually his cousin, he raised her as his daughter. When Mordecai spoke a word he expected her to listen and obey because he was preparing Esther for her destiny. If she didn't listen and obey God would give the privilege of delivering the people to someone else.

Before Esther could spend the night with the king she had to go through a time of purification and sweetening in the anointing of myrrh. For one whole year Esther was cleansed and prepared just to spend one night with the king. This night was a very important one for Esther and her people, the Jews. She was not going to have a night at the door of the king without having the anointing on her and in her. She endured a year of processing before even making an appointment to see the king.

Are you anointed? Have you spent the necessary time bathing in the fragrance, fruit and gifts of the spirit? It may seem like a long, drawn-out process, but committing to your preparation is important. I know you desperately want to be married, but are you willing to endure the process by following the guidelines of Mordecai (the Holy Ghost) and become anointed?

> *Wherewithal shall a young man cleanse his way? by taking heed thereto according to thy word.*

> *Psalm 119:9 (KJV)*

Before You Can Lie with Your King, You Must Be Anointed

Do You Have a Mentor?

> *Now unto him that is able to do exceeding abundantly above all that we ask or think, according to the power that worketh in us, unto him be glory in the church by Christ Jesus throughout all ages, world without end. Amen.*
>
> *Ephesians 3:20-21 (KJV)*

Before You Can Lie with Your King, You Must Be Anointed

A Father's Words and Blessing

A Father's Words

You have heard directly from the heart of a spiritual father, not a lustful heart (because you are my daughters, the handiwork of the Lord). My heart is one of protection and covering for my daughters from wolves and dogs and the pain they bring (Acts 20:29). If you have **seriously examined yourself** and earnestly sought the salvation, deliverance, and strength of the Lord then you have graduated from the former state of mind you had when first beginning the journey through these pages. It is time to move forward into the blessing Jesus has reserved for you from the foundation of the world. Before I end this book I want to give a father's blessing and release you into the hands of the man of God who will be your husband. Lift up your spiritual hands and receive these words.

So now my daughter, after receiving Jesus Christ as your Lord and Savior on top the instruction, revelation and word of knowledge in this book and receiving the fragrances of the Lord Jesus, I now bless you to be found by the man of God who will be your husband.

- All your former curses are canceled.
- Your broken heart is mended.
- Your blinded eyes are opened.
- Your confusion is now a sound mind.
- Your disease is now comforted (healed)
- Your low places are now high and your proud attitude has fallen.
- Your loneliness has now been filled with God's chosen – No more lonely days.

This I decree In Jesus' name

Before You Can Lie with Your King, You Must Be Anointed

A Father's Blessing

May your years be long and your days sweet.
May your joy overflow like a mighty river.
May you be given your heart's desire for a husband and family.

> *May the LORD bless you and keep you. May the LORD make His face to shine upon you, and be gracious to you. The LORD lift up His countenance upon you, and give you peace.*
>
> *Numbers 6:24-26*

Research and references were obtained from the following sources:

Enhanced Brown-Driver-Briggs
Hebrew and English Lexicon
Enhanced Strong's Lexicon
Harper's Bible Dictionary
New American Standard, Updated Edition Exhaustive Concordance
**   of the Bible**
New Bible Dictionary, Third Edition
New Nave's Topical Bible
Victorie-Inc. (www.victorie-inc.us)

TOPIC INDEX

E

El Elyon, 104, *See* GOD
Elijah, 36, 143, 144, 153
En-gedi, 38, 138
Er, 130, 131, 132
Esther, 197, 198, 199, 200
Eve, 21, 82, 119, 120, 159,
  160, 161, 164, 165, 167

F

faith, 16, 33, 34, 40, 48, 53, 58,
  60, 64, 73, 76, 81, 88, 98,
  116, 144, 147, 149, 166, 168,
  192
fellowship, 19, 20, 66
female, 16, 17, 18, 70, 78, 117,
  186
fins, 142, 147, 149, 153
fish, 142, 143, 144, 145, 146,
  147, 148, 149, 150, 151, 152,
  153
flies, 123, 174, 175, 176, 177,
  178, 179, 180, 181, 182, 183,
  184, 185, 187, 188, 189
foolishness, 26, 40, 45, 121,
  174, 176, 178, 194, 195
fornication, 87, 163, 166, 180,
  187, 193
fragrance haters, 122, 123, 125,
  128, 129, 130, 132, 133
frankincense, *See under* nine
  spiritual fragrances
funk, 122, 145, 178

G

garden, 31, 116, 117, 118, 155,
  185, 186, 188
Garden of Eden, 19, 20, 118,
  119, 120, 159, 160, 164, 165
gentleness, *See under* nine
  spiritual fruits
GOD, 16, 17, 18, 19, 20, 21,
  22, 23, 25, 26, 27, 29, 30, 35,
  36, 38, 39, 40, 41, 42, 43, 44,
  47, 48, 50, 51, 53, 55, 56, 58,
  59, 61, 62, 64, 66, 67, 68, 71,
  72, 73, 74, 75, 76, 77, 78, 79,
  80, 81, 82, 85, 87, 90, 91, 92,
  93, 94, 95, 96, 98, 103, 104,
  105, 106, 108, 111, 112, 113,
  116, 117, 118, 119, 120, 122,
  123, 124, 125, 128, 129, 130,
  131, 132, 133, 134, 135, 136,
  138, 139, 140, 141, 143, 144,
  145, 146, 147, 148, 149, 150,
  151, 152, 153, 154, 155, 157,
  158, 159, 160, 161, 162, 163,
  165, 166, 168, 169, 170, 174,
  175, 176, 177, 178, 179, 180,
  181, 182, 187, 188, 189, 191,
  192, 193, 194, 195, 196, 199,
  200, 202
God-Man, 93
goodness, *See under* nine
  spiritual fruits

H

harvest of men, 75, 76, 77, 78,
  80

Books, Messages, Prayers and Prophecies on DVD and CD are available online:

www.spiritualfragrance.org

TITLE	DVD	CD
Weapons For Your Strong Holds	$15	$7
Help Kids Are Off The Hook		$7
The Marriage Partnership		$7
Cover Your Father's Mistakes		$7
How To Carry A Prayer		$7
The Northeaster (*The Battle For Your Destiny*)		$7
The Priestly Blessing		$7
Teen Dating		$7
The Spiritual Fragrance of a Woman, Revival #1	$15	$7
The Spiritual Fragrance of a Woman, Revival #2	$15	$7

To invite Pastor Davison to minister at your
worship service, conference, or special event, please contact:

Jerone Davison Ministries
Attention: Lana Henry
600 Kentucky Street
P.O. Box 3463
Fairfield, CA 94534
(707) 435-8077

Or visit www.spiritualfragrance.org .

Thank You